FRACTURED PARADISE

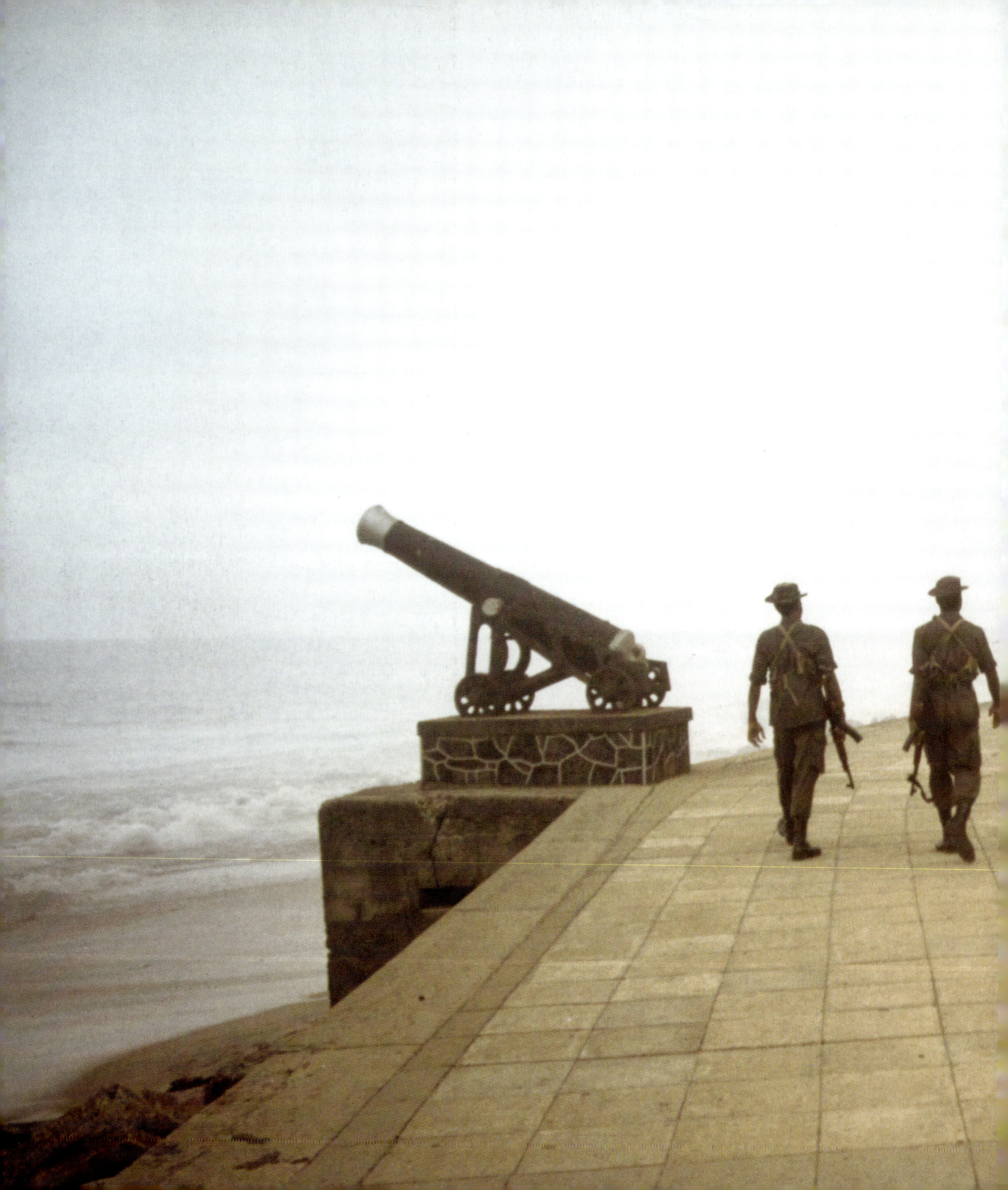

Paul Harris

FRACTURED PARADISE
Images of Sri Lanka

a Frontline book

In praise of serendipity . . .
for my friends in Sri Lanka

First published in the United Kingdom 2001
by Frontline Publications
Whittingehame House
Haddington
EH41 4QA

email: publisher@conflictanalysis.com

Pictures and text © copyright Paul Harris 2001

ISBN: 0-9540640-0-3 (paperback)
      0-9540640-1-1 (hardback)

All rights reserved. No part of this book may be reproduced or transmitted in any form or by any means, electronic or mechanical, including photocopy, recording or any other information storage and retrieval system existing or hereinafter invented, without prior permission in writing from Frontline Publications.

Photoprocessing by Pyramid, Edinburgh
Cameras by Nikon, Contax and Fuji
Text and repro by Syntax, Edinburgh, Scotland
Printed on Nopacoat 135gsm matt art supplied by Europapier, Ljubljana

Printed by Delo Tiskarna in the Republic of Slovenia by arrangement with Korotan, Ljubljana

CONTENTS

Colombo

Jaffna

Batti & Trinco

People

Enduring Images

Introduction

Mark Twain arrived in Colombo on January 13 1896. The famous American writer, travelling around the world following the Equator, was instantly enchanted with Ceylon. "Dear me, it is beautiful," he wrote. "And most sumptuously tropical, as to character of foliage and opulence of it . . . oriental charm and mystery and tropical deliciousness . . . There was that swoon in the air which one associates with the tropics, and that smother of heat, heady with odours of unknown flowers, and that sudden invasion of purple gloom fissured with lightning, ten the tumult of crashing thunder and the downpour – and presently all sunny and smiling again; all these things were there; the conditions were complete, nothing was lacking . . .".

All the beauty and charm remains in modern Sri Lanka but the publicity has taken its inevitable toll: the news of bomb blasts, battlefield reverses and security clampdowns. The mass of tourists stay away and the undoubted attractions of Sri Lanka are visited by just a dedicated and enlightened few. There must be at least a dozen good reasons to visit Sri Lanka - breathtaking scenery, ancient sites, wonderful beaches, wildlife, birds, arts and crafts, unpolluted crystal-white beaches and opportunities for underwater exploration.

Actually, there are around half a million foreign tourists a year travelling to Sri Lanka soaking up locations as diverse as the 6th century fortress of Sigiriya, on a 600 foot rock which rises sheer from the jungle; the vast temple complexes of Polonnaruwa and Anaradhapura; the Dalada Maligawa in Kandy; tea plantations in the cool of the hills of the central highlands; and the elephant orphanage at Pinnawela.

The first western travellers perceived what is today known as Sri Lanka, with its luscious landscapes, white beaches, smiling, graceful inhabitants and the bounteous fruit of the trees, as a paradise on earth. Sri Lanka is, indeed, a place of beauty, charm and startling paradoxes. Marco Polo thought it the 'the finest island of its size in the world'. This little piece of paradise was known to the British as Ceylon; to the Romans as Taprobane; to the Dutch as Ceylan; and to Muslim traders as Serendib, the island of serendipity. The local minority Tamil population called it Eelam and the majority Sinhalese restored their own historical name Sri Lanka in 1972. It is at once all things to all men and one mighty enigma: beautiful, baffling and seductive, this land of gently swaying palms, golden beaches and ancient temples has sadly seen extraordinary violence.

A land of paradoxes, may they shortly be resolved.

Paul Harris, April 2001

Colombo

I was but three days into my first visit to Sri Lanka...

It was almost a quarter to eleven on the morning of Wednesday January 31 1996 in the teeming business quarter of the Sri Lankan capital, Colombo: a warm and overcast 31 degrees. Two vehicles were closing on the main thoroughfare, travelling separately: a trishaw, the open three-wheeler so popular locally, and a large yellow, wooden-sided lorry ostensibly piled with 40 bags of rice husks.

Opposite the forecourt of the Intercontinental Hotel, two men left the trishaw with short cylindrical bundles under their arms. The lorry stopped in the clearly marked 'Towing Zone' at the front entrance of the Central Bank next to the security barrier. Immediately, security guards in light-brown uniforms, armed with ancient single barrel 12-bore shotguns, stepped forward to move the truck on, but, as they did so, two men dressed in traditional sarongs leapt from their positions perched on sacks of rice in the back of the truck. Both opened fire with Chinese manufactured T56 automatic rifles scattering the security guards.

Meantime, the two men from the trishaw had reached the Ceylinco Building, twenty or thirty yards down the road and the headquarters of the country's principal insurance company. As the commotion started at the bank across the road, and, in a pre-planned diversionary tactic, one of the trishaw attackers unwrapped his bundle to reveal it to be a single-use, disposable rocket launcher. He shouldered and launched a missile through a window on the third floor of the building, which ignited almost immediately and flames leapt from the window.

Meantime, across the road, the driver of the lorry was repeatedly ramming the barrier at the front of the bank, reversing back and then trying again. This went on for fully three minutes. Police in the area took cover as soon as the fighting started, security guards fled, and although guards from the nearby Navy Headquarters building engaged the terrorists in fire, they also retreated after two were shot and killed.

Unable to break through into the main foyer of the building, the driver left his cab, detonated an electric charge fixed to his 'suicide jacket' and blew the lorry's cargo: an estimated 400 kgs of high explosive.

The blast of the explosion destroyed every single building on both sides of the road; the whole length of the main street of the commercial quarter. Some 300 yards of frontage and twelve major buildings were destroyed in the explosion. All around the interiors of the buildings caught fire as electrics shorted and dozens of cars, trishaws and vans burned. Almost a hundred people had died, either crushed by rubble or burned alive and 1,400 were soon on their way to hospital. Within minutes of the explosion Colombo seized up as army trucks, police, ambulances and rescue services converged on the commercial area. I abandoned my car and ran for just over ten minutes into a maelstrom of fire, debris and death.

In the area of the explosion in those minutes following, visibility was reduced almost to zero. Thick black smoke billowed everywhere and through the thick choking, fog flames roared from windows, the heat searing your skin. On the edge of the commercial district, bedroom windows in the Intercontinental Hotel were shattered and the curtains flapped uselessly in the gentle breeze.

And the blood. In the 30 degree heat the blood was already dry on the pavements like pools of crimson sealing wax.

All around milled the injured, the merely curious and the aimless. Police, army, navy and RAF personnel, Special Task Force police, sailors in crisp white uniforms from the nearby Navy HQ, bomb disposal squads, commandos from the Airborne Division. There were even a few firemen. But turntable ladders and snorkels were not to arrive for more than an hour after the explosion and by one o'clock the Sri Lankan airforce was dropping water bombs all over the blazing centre: Bell Huey helicopters scooping up water from the lake in front of the nearby parliament buildings and then dumping it in great curling showers from the sky.

All eyes at one point were turned to a window high up on

the Ceylinco building. Two bloodied men, their clothes hanging in rags around them climbed onto the ledge of their window. You could see why: the flames shot out through the aperture behind them and they made to jump - just as part of the Central Bank collapsed behind me with a deep rumling roar. Everbody sprinted for cover as debris showered down. I looked back at the window but the figures were gone.

A couple of hours later the police dug the body of one of the terrorists out of the rubble at the front of the bank. I've never seen a body quite like it. It immediately reminded me - rather ludicrously - of the bad taste joke about the man run over by a steamroller: they slipped him under the hospital door. This man no longer resembled an example of humanity: he was as flat as the proverbial pancake. "Tamil bastard," spat the policeman. He was, in fact, just one of the sarong clad terrorists thought to number five or six who had driven a truck packed with explosives up to the front door of the bank.

Seven hours later, as night fell in Colombo, smoke still rose from the shattered business heart of this Asian capital. A city centre curfew was imposed, there was a city wide appeal for blood donors and hospital staff, and the Department of Information was appealing for calm.

Fortunately, I was a few hundred yards down the road when the bomb blew. I could see, through the car window, the plume of thick black smoke rising hundreds of feet into the air. At the time the separatist Tamil Tiger rebels struck the heart of the Sri Lankan capital, I was just leaving the splendid and anachronistic colonial splendour of the Galle Face Hotel.

The promise of the letterhead is amply fulfilled: 'Established 1864. Dedicated to Yesterday's Charm and Tomorrow's Comfort'. Known to its fans simply as 'the GFH', one writer aptly referred to it as 'a colonial time machine'.

It must be difficult to find a hotel anywhere in the world so redolent of the charms of yesteryear. More of a colonial-style palace than a hotel, aged retainers in pristine white military-style uniforms, replete with red epaulettes and gold braid, cheerily salute your progress through the magnificent, airy halls and over the creaking teak floors and fraying red carpets. Many of them have worked in the hotel for more than half a century. The ratio of staff to guests is a generous four to one. No employee has ever been sacked, apparently.

But, on your way to your room, you do note the first signs of a certain eccentricity but are just mildly amused. Notices on the stairs like 'Silence is Golden' seem a trifle quaint.

'Galle Face Hotel admires your decision not smoke', implies a laudable concern for your health. A notice advising a room discount of $10 a night if you refrain from smoking indeed seems rather generous. 'Please do not smoke in bed because the ashes we find might be yours' is a little more threatening and the one beside the lift, 'Please walk down. It's good for your health,' strikes you as just a little impertinent.

Your bedroom, furnished with genuine, highly polished antiques, will likely be the size of half a dozen modern chain hotel rooms put together: the average size seems to be around 30 foot by 20 foot. And all for less than fifty dollars a night . . . The King Emperor Suite, which has oft housed members of the British Royal family, is said to have the largest lounge in any hotel anywhere in the world.

It is a real seaside hotel: the waves break onto the beach just a few yards from your window, beyond the neatly manicured lawns. To my mind, the best thing about the Galle Face is sitting on the terrace of an early evening with a gin and tonic watching the fiery red sun setting slowly into the Indian Ocean beyond the gently stirring coconut palms.

It seems there was a time when anybody who was anybody would stay at the GFH when in Ceylon. Alec Guinness relaxed here after filming *Bridge over the River Kwai* up country. A bust of Arthur C Clarke sprouted in the main hall a few years ago. Clarke has finished several of his books in seclusion in one of the suites of the hotel, most lately *3001: The Final Oddyssey*. Beside the bust stands a stone water trough topped with frangipani petals. Birds freely nesting in the rafters above can swoop down to drink. Film-makers often come to the hotel to shoot movies. One Italian director told me, "Everything is here, untouched. We save all the money on the set budget". More recently, the hotel was the setting for a wonderful novel, Looking out to Sea by Peter Adamson.

The plaques and notices are effectively memorials to the hotel's eccentric owner, now deceased, Major Cyril Gardiner. Often charming, frequently uncompromising if not totally intransigent, Gardiner was a true autocrat within his own four walls. Gardiner gave a lunch in the hotel for the Queen of Denmark - after whom he named a suite - and after the meal she noticed a No Smoking sign. Though reportedly "craving" a cigarette even the Royal Personage forbore to smoke in Gardiner's forbidding presence.

The GFH embodies all those paradoxes of ancient Ceylon and modern Sri Lanka; old and new jostling uneasily together. It is a combination of disarming charm

The Central Bank burns two hours after the bomb blast.

January 31 1996.

and inefficiency; authoritariansim and servility, good humoured chaos and occasional breakdowns in the human relationship.

A few years ago, Cyril, before he died on the dance floor of the Galle Face Hotel, appointed a newly retired army Brigadier to run the hotel. The ill-remunerated, long suffering staff took to the street outside the hotel to noisily demonstrate with banners. Senior management duly took over the essential running of the hotel. A friend of mine working in a rather senior position in the army had a telephone call from the beleagured Brigadier warning of imminent revolution on the streets of Colombo. A group of army officers donned civilian clothes and went down to sort matters out, with force if necessary. As my friend the General puts it, "It was certainly a noisy demonstration but when we saw the banners we fell about laughing. They protested 'Yesterday a Brigadier, today a dishwasher'. These fellows clearly had a sense of humour and couldn't be a serious threat to anybody. We had a few beers and went home." Good humour won the day on that occasion.

Cyril has passed on to the great hotel in the sky after a heart attack on the GFH dance floor but his spirit remains. The telephones are unpredictable. The fax goes down for two or three days at a time. A uniformed servant smilingly presents you with a telephone message written in beautiful script.

As you tip him 50 rupees you discern the message is three days old. Breakfast on the terrace is a leisurely affair. The bill can take twenty minutes to materialise. The coffee is legendary. Quite undrinkable. There is no bar to stand at - Cyril was a teetotaller but drinks are served to table by waiters in starched sarongs. Cyril once admitted. "This hotel is not perfect but I think it is delightfully imperfect." The actress Carrie Fisher wrote to Gardiner summing up the appeal of his establishment, "You could be alone here without ever feeling lonely."

As security forces and emergency services cleared up as best they could in the wake of the devastation caused by the Central Bank blast, Industrial Development Minister C V Gooneratne visited Fort to see the situation for himself. He must have felt deep, inner dismay but he declared that he would not be defeated by the LTTE and that the Fort business district would be rebuilt. In a bitter twist of irony, in June 2000, as Fort rose from the ashes, he himself would die, the victim of a suicide bomber in Ratmalana, his own Colombo constituency.

The LTTE first pioneered the technology of the suicide bomber. This they have developed, honed and exported all over the world. Lt Col Susantha Seneanyake vividly recalls the events of July 4 1997. That is hardly surprising. It was the day he found the head of the female suicide bomber who had blown herself apart: it was all that was left of her. She destroyed her own life and those of 22 others in a carefully premeditated attack on the Sri Lankan Housing Minister, who was visiting Jaffna to coordinate reconstruction in the wake of being retaken by government forces. The Housing Minister survived but the military commander, Maj Gen Ananda Hamangoda, soldiers and local civilians were killed by the explosives contained in a suicide waistcoat worn by the woman underneath her blouse next to her skin.

"I remember she was an ugly woman." He goes on. "I always tell my men to look out for ugly women or those with poor complexions. After all, a beautiful woman has everything to live for. She's not going to blowing herself up, is she ?" This potted philosophy may be neither politically correct nor the absolute truth of the matter but it does prompt the question as to what type of woman carries out such an attack.

Out of the total Tiger strength of some 14,000 cadres it is estimated that around 4,000 are women. Like their male counterparts, they are organised in a cell structure across a range of specialised activities. The crack infantry are organised in what are known as Black Tiger units. Within the Black Tigers are sea units and suicide units and it is known that many of these units are made up of women. The crack suicide units are known as 'Karum Puligal'. Not all the women fight - some are in medical and supplies units or in the political or students' wings - but those who do have earned a reputation for their single-minded toughness and determination, and none so much as the female suicide bomber unit.

The Liberation Tigers of Tamil Eelam (LTTE) have developed and perfected the suicide waistcoat as a particularly deadly form of attack. According to Colombo academic Rohan Gunaratne, who has made an extensive study of the LTTE in Sri Lanka and the United States, they are "technologically the most sophisticated terrorist group in the world." They pioneered the technology of the suicide bomb and are widely believed to be technically more advanced than better known groups like Hamas and Hizbollah. Gunaratne believes the LTTE sold the suicide jacket technology to Hizbollah - possibly in a trade for weapons and training - and they have successfully used it against Israeli military targets, both within Israel and in the

Lebanon. The suicide jacket is essentially a bomb kit worn as a waistcoat next to the skin, fashioned from canvas and with plastic explosives and detonator secreted in four pockets. It has been at its most deadly when utilised by female cadres of the LTTE.

On May 21 1991, Dhanu, an LTTE human bomb, destroyed herself, Indian Prime Minister Rajiv Gandhi and 16 others near Madras in protest against India's 1987-90 military intervention in Jaffna, regarded as the heartland of the Tigers. This is the only recorded use of the suicide bomber in India, outside Kashmir. In 1994, Opposition leader and Presidential candidate Gamini Dissanayake, and some 50 other people, were killed by a female suicide bomber at a packed political meeting on the outskirts of the Sri Lankan capital, Colombo. On May 1 1993, President Premadasa was killed in a blast at a political rally. In February 1998, a female bomber blew herself up outside air force headquarters in central Colombo, killing nine people, shortly after Prince Charles' aircraft took off from the aurport. In December 1999, President Kumaratunga was herself targeted by a female suicide bomber at an election rally: 34 people died and the President lost her eye. And in June 2000, C V Gooneratne, his wife and 23 others were killed by a suicide bomber as he met his constitutents in a southern Colombo suburb: the dead included no less than ten security men accompanying the minister.

This is just a mini-catalogue of the grim harvest of the suicide bomber. According to sources in the security

Victim of the Central Bank bomb.

services, between 1987 and November 2000 there were 153 suicide attacks in Sri Lanka. Around 1,200 civilians, soldiers and political leaders died in these attacks, including 148 bombers. Thirty-nine provincial and national Tamil leaders have been killed by the LTTE. Interestingly, the very same day as Gooneratne died, suicide bombers mounted an attack for the first time in Chechnya against a Russian military target. Security experts believe the LTTE has been in contact with the Chechen guerillas and are in the process of a technology transfer. On July 3 2000, Chechen suicide bombers were reported to have killed at least 37 Russian soldiers and innjured scores of others in a series of blasts at five different locations in Chechnya. At Argun, on the outskirts of the capital of Grozny, a truck laden with explosives crashed through the gate of a hostel housing police troops killing 27. And just a few weeks later, the US warship Cole would be attacked in the Yemeni port of Aden by suicide bombers who killed 17 US sailors and occasioned critical damage to the ship. Three days before that attack, LTTE suicide bombers attacked Sri Lanka navy ships in the port of Trincomalee. The style and methodolgy of attack was identical . . .

The records show that the bombers employ one of three basic means to carry out their deadly trade: the suicide waistcoat worn next to the skin; the bicycle with its metal tubing packed with plastic explosive; and the truck packed with explosives, which is driven right into the target by a suicide bomber-driver. The most spectacular example of this last method was the attack on Colombo's financial district on January 31 1996. Equally spectacular, although not so devastating in terms of loss of life, was the 1998 attack, immediately prior to the visit of HRH The Prince of Wales to Sri Lanka, was the truck bomb attack on the most holy Buddhist shrine in the town of Kandy, the Dalada Maligawa.

The very first truck bomb was driven by a cadre immortalised in LTTE mythology as Captain Miller. On July 5 1987 he drove a truck laden with explosives into a Jaffna school killing 128 soldiers of the Gajaba Regiment. He was immortalised by the LTTE with wall posters all over Jaffna.

The bicycle bomb is more commonly used in the east and has been used several times in the Batticaloa region, including an attack on the bus station there. It is essentially a less sophisticated mechanism and does not cause such a devastating blast.

Sometimes it is unclear as to whether the bomber has died in the blast. Such an example was the Dehiwala train bomb in July 1996. Twin blasts on an evening commuter train killed 57 people. It was unclear whether a bomber aboard the train triggered the blasts, and died in the process, or it was effected from a nearby location like the railway bridge at the station.

Some of the bombers are men. They appear to be motivated by devout political commitment; devotion to their leader, Prabhakaran. That commitment appears cult-like. Within the LTTE he is all powerful and all pervasive. This devotion to the cause and the man is reinforced by Martyrs' Weeks, creation of heroes' cemeteries and the naming of weapons after those who give up their lives. There is said to be the chance of dining with Prabhakran on the day of passing out as a suicide bomber. For those who then lay down the their lives there is the promise of martyrdom.

However, most suicide attacks are effected by female bombers. Why the female ? It is difficult practically and, indeed, culturally for male soldiers or police to frisk, never mind conduct body searches of women. And so, whilst all men passing through Sri Lanka's ubiquitous checkpoints are thoroughly searched, the women go through on the nod with just a cursory handbag search, except for a very small number where there are women officers to conduct more intimate body searches.

Colombo-based writer and researcher Mangalika de Silva, who is also the Sri Lanka coordinator of Women for Peace, says there is a logicality to using women as suicide bombers. "In a public place a woman may seem less threatening. She has the edge to use the situation most effectively. It is part of the LTTE war strategy to inflict the maximum damage."

In recent years, women fighters have joined the LTTE struggle for an independent Tamil state in significant numbers. LTTE leader Vellupillai Prabhakaran, an old style Marxist-Leninist type of revolutionary leader, brought women into the fighting wing of his movement during the late 1980s. Mangalika de Silva believes that this was not on account of their burning revolutionary spirit, or because they were necessarily better fighters than men. Instead, she explains, "As an overwhelming number of male cadres were killed in battle, this anomaly created a situation where recruitment of women became a necessity."

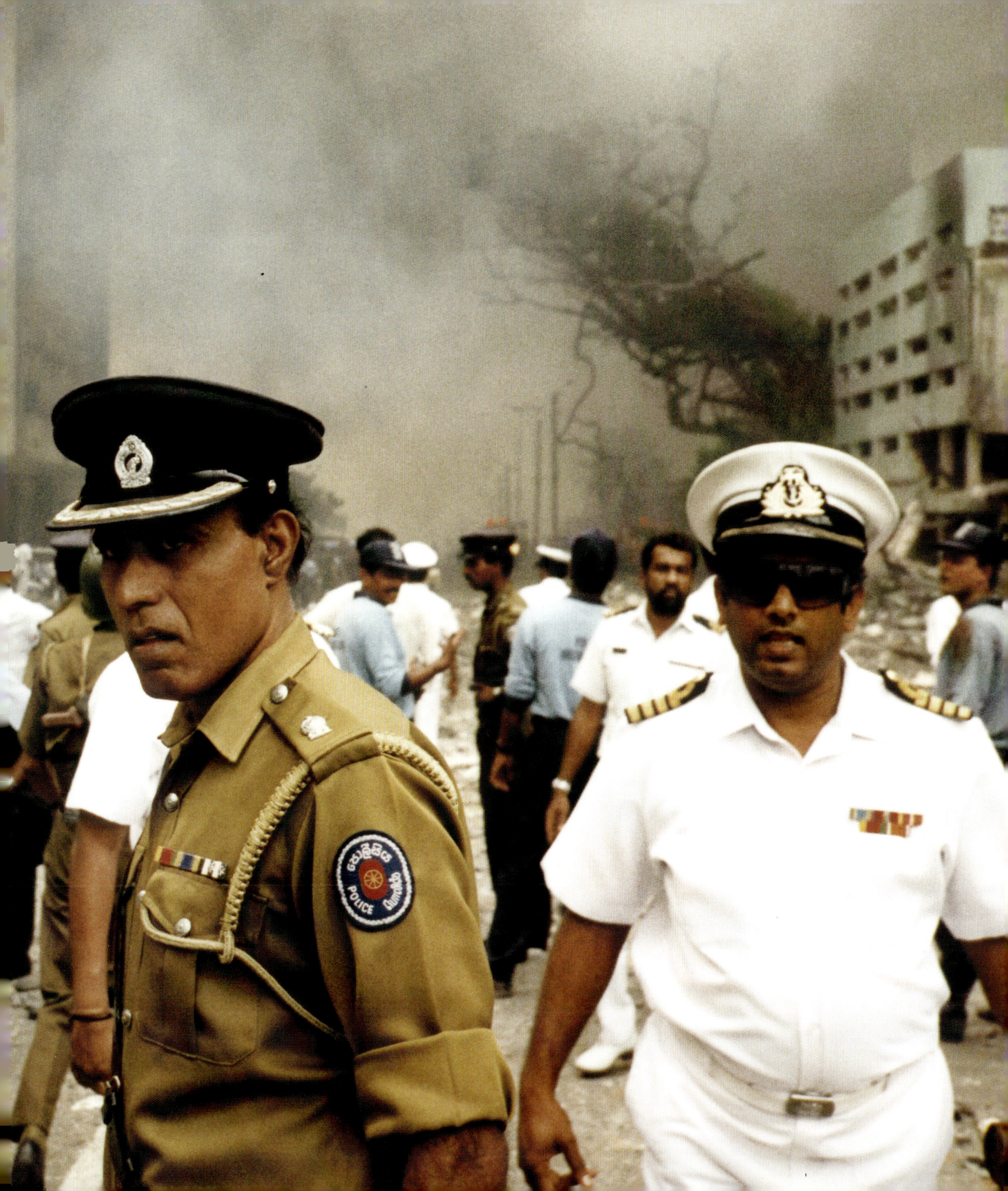
POLICE

The Ceylinco Building burns across the road from the Central Bank.

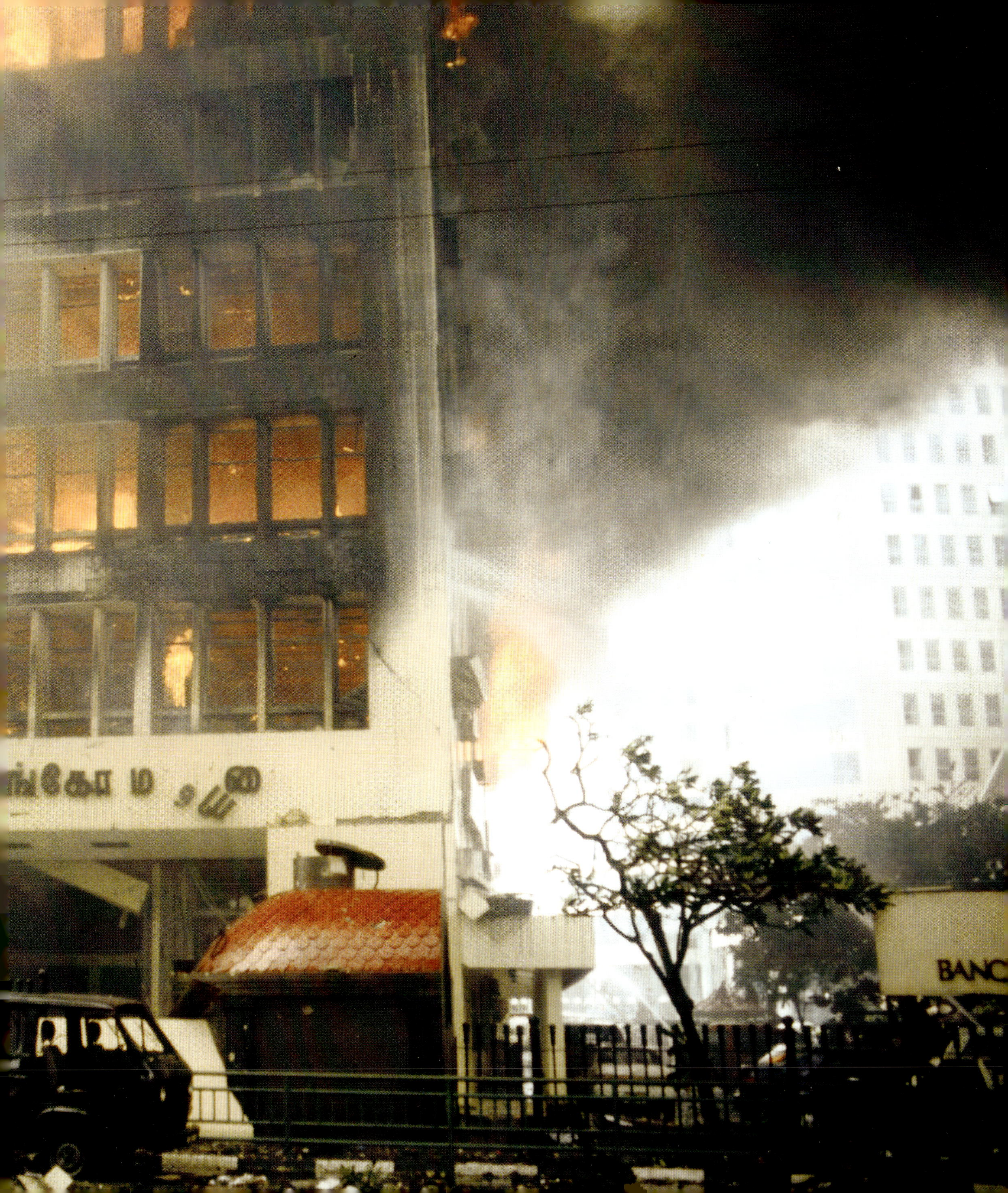
BANC

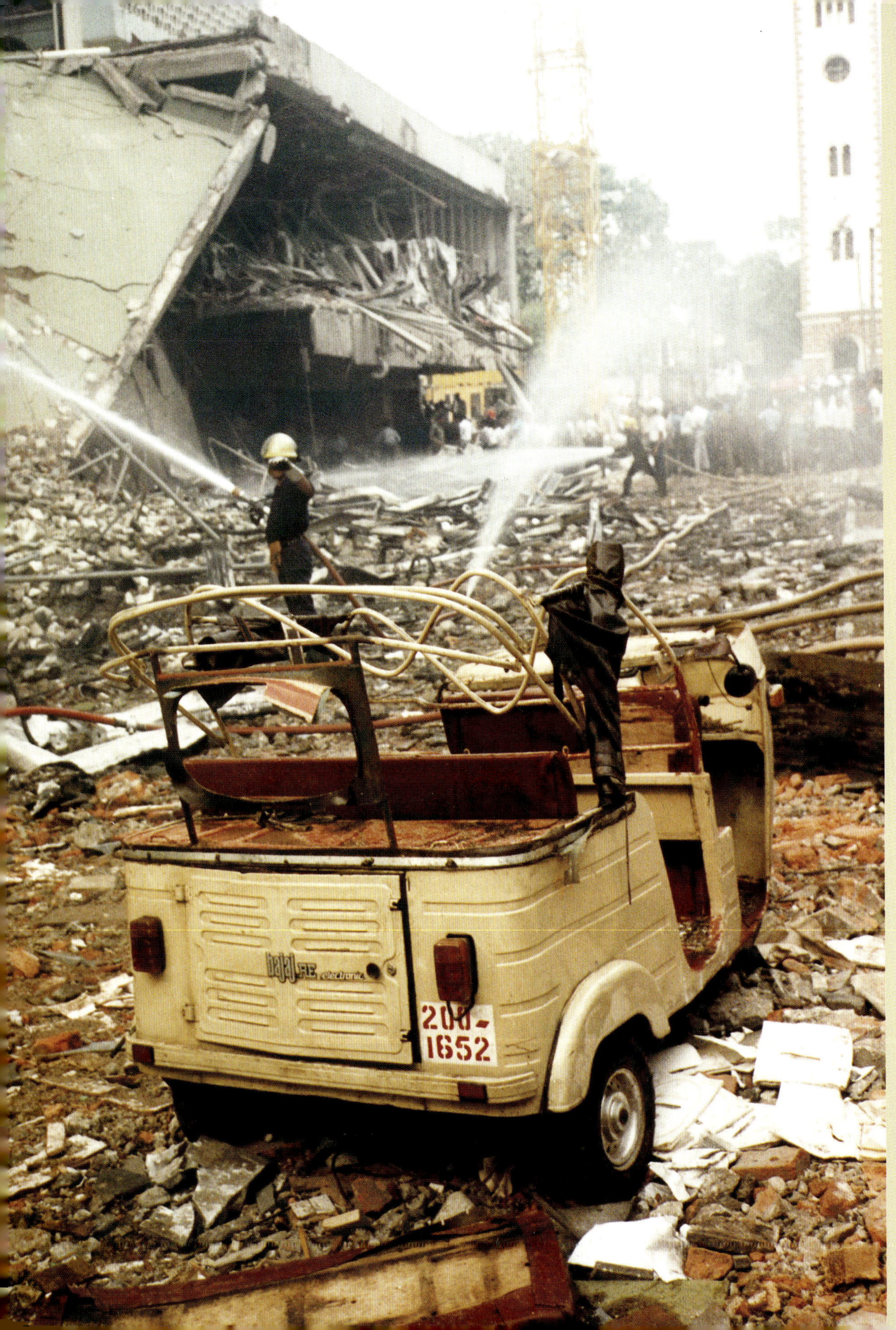
200-
1652

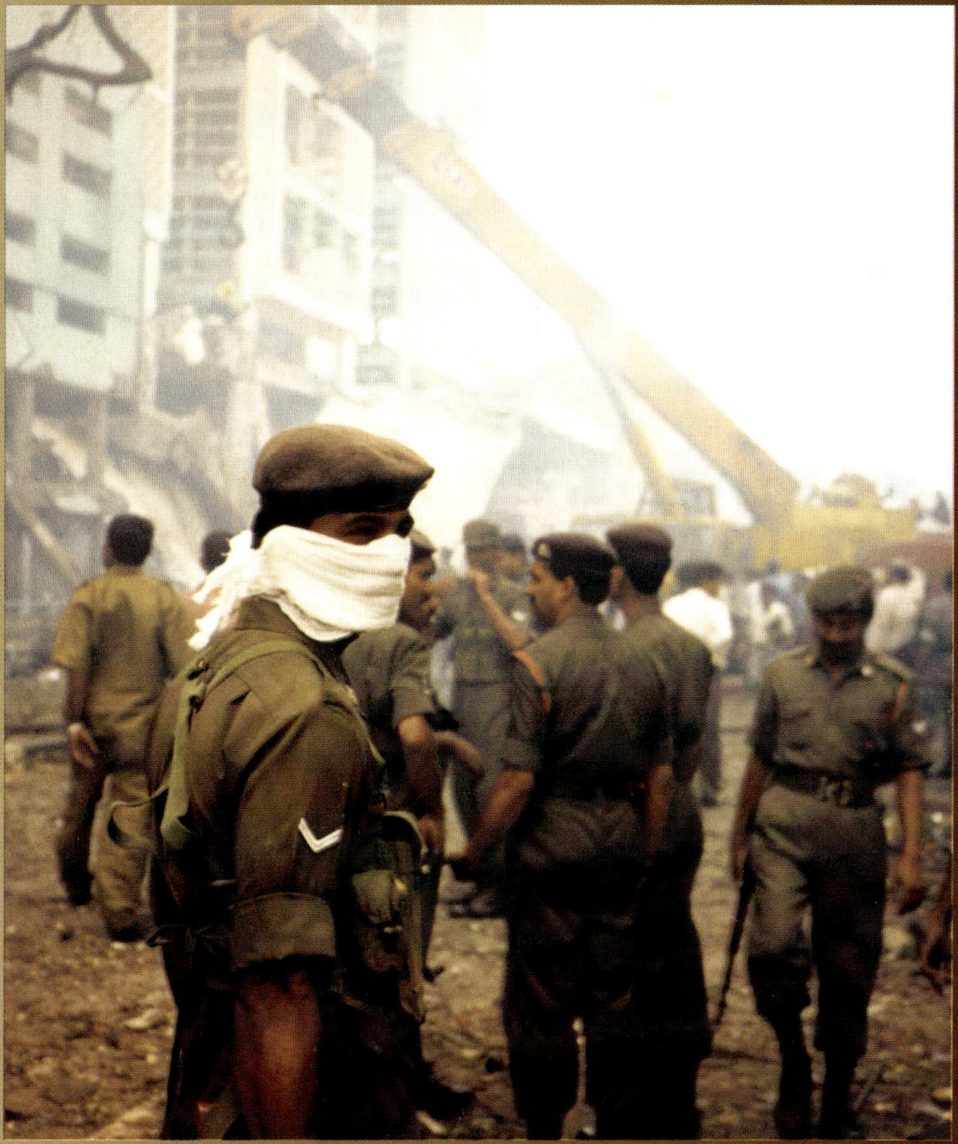

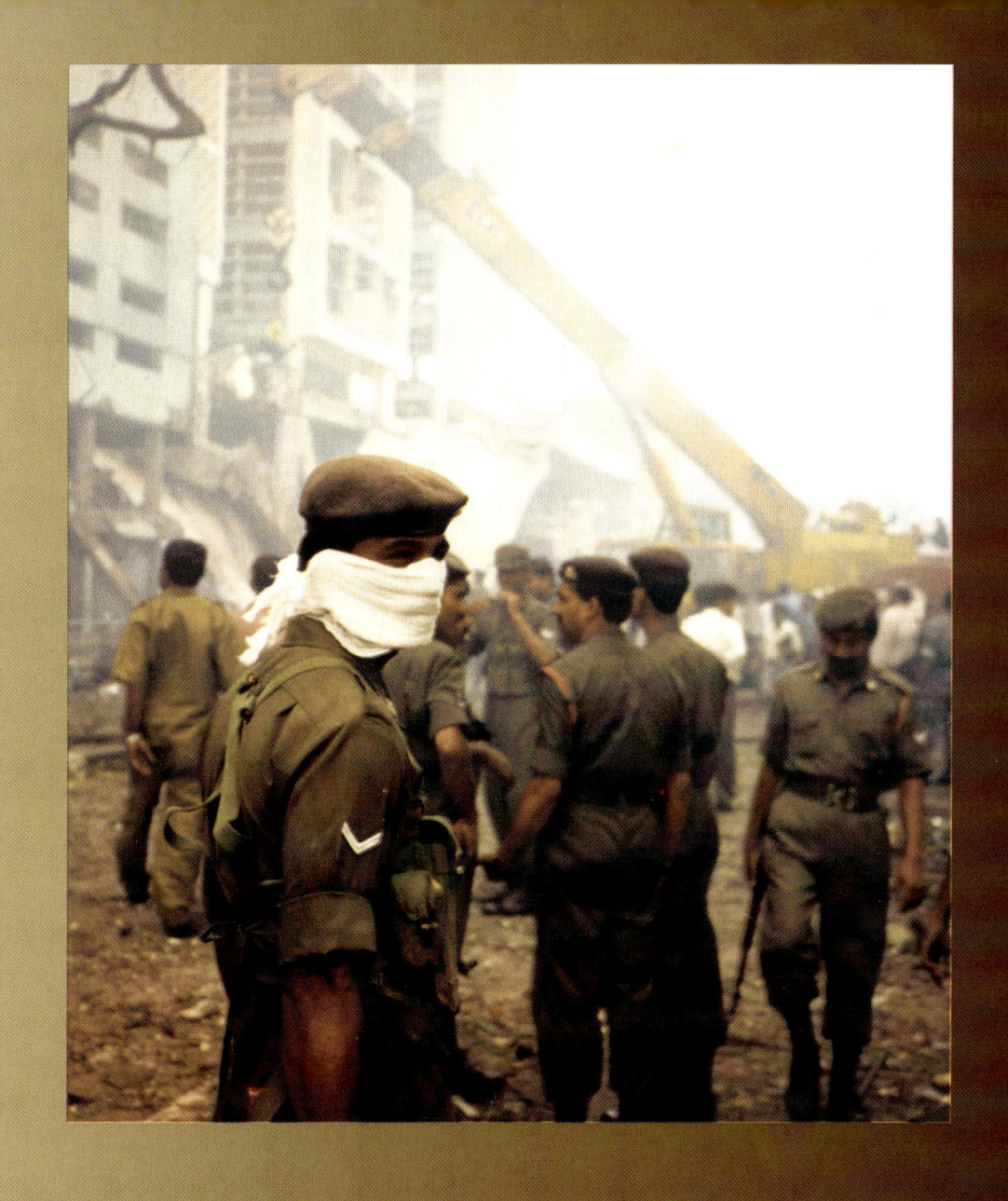

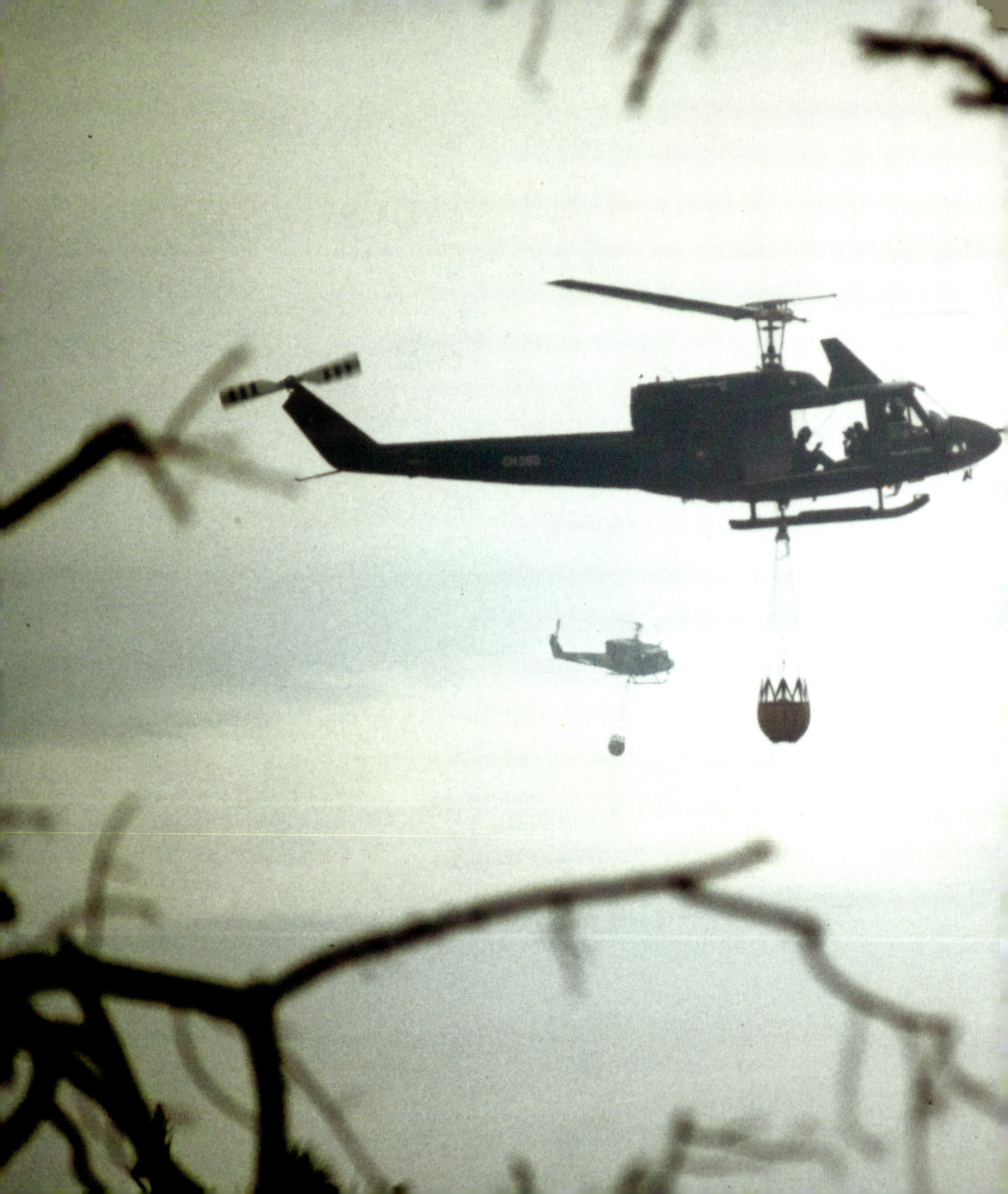

Bell Huey helicopters approach the centre of Colombo to dump water on blazing buildings.

The view down Galle Green an hour after the blast.
Smoke envelops the Fort district, the commercial area of Colombo.

This elegant, sari-clad woman stood out in sharp contrast to the devastation and mayhem all around her.

The Dehiwala train blast.

Two explosions rocked the rush hour commuter train out of the city as it drew into Dehiwala Station. The explosions were simultaneous raising the possibility of remotely controlled blasts.

Fifty-seven passengers died in the crowded, confined space of the train.

July 24 1996.

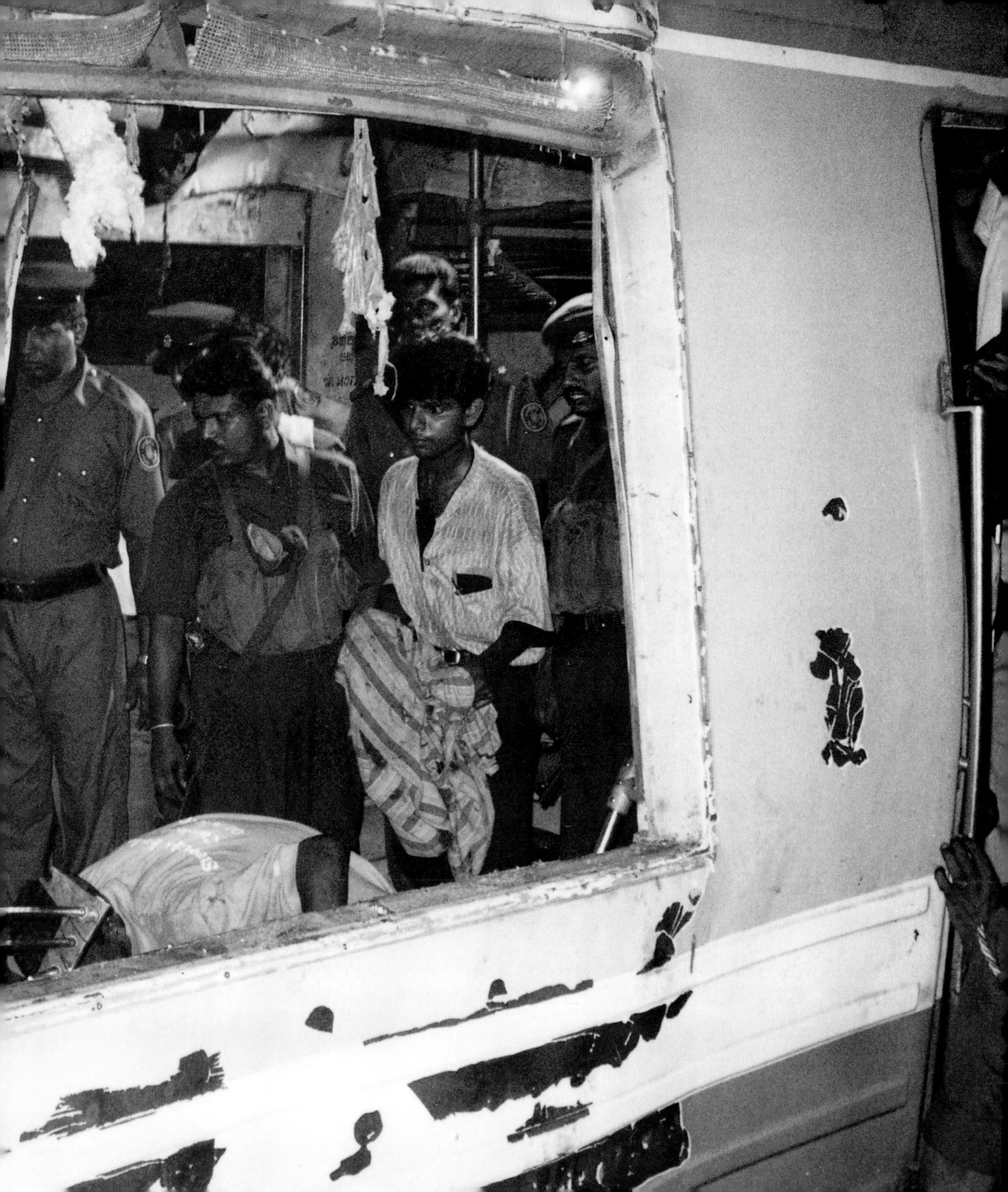

Bicycle bomb blast at Wattala on the road to the airport. *July 2000.*

Police question witnesses below the serene statue of the Lord Buddha at the scene of the bicycle bomb explosion at Wattala. A Sri Lanka Air Force bus was passing at the time of the explosion and it was initially believed to have been an attack on the bus. It later transpired that the bicycle, with explosives packed into its crossbar, may have unwittingly been stolen by the rider and then remotely detonated by a terrorist.

Alternatively, the LTTE may have engaged a Sinhala man to carry out the attack

The great escape. Soldiers Weerasinghe Devalage Weerasinghe (right) and Lunuwila Aratchige Mahinda Kumara (left) escaped when their unit was overrun in Elephant Pass in April 2000. They survived against all odds behind enemy lines for nine months and ten days before making it back to headquarters. Despite sustaining shrapnel injuries and four bullet wounds between them, they managed to survive on coconuts, the roots of young palmyrah trees, wild ginger, ditch water and their own urine. *March 2001*.

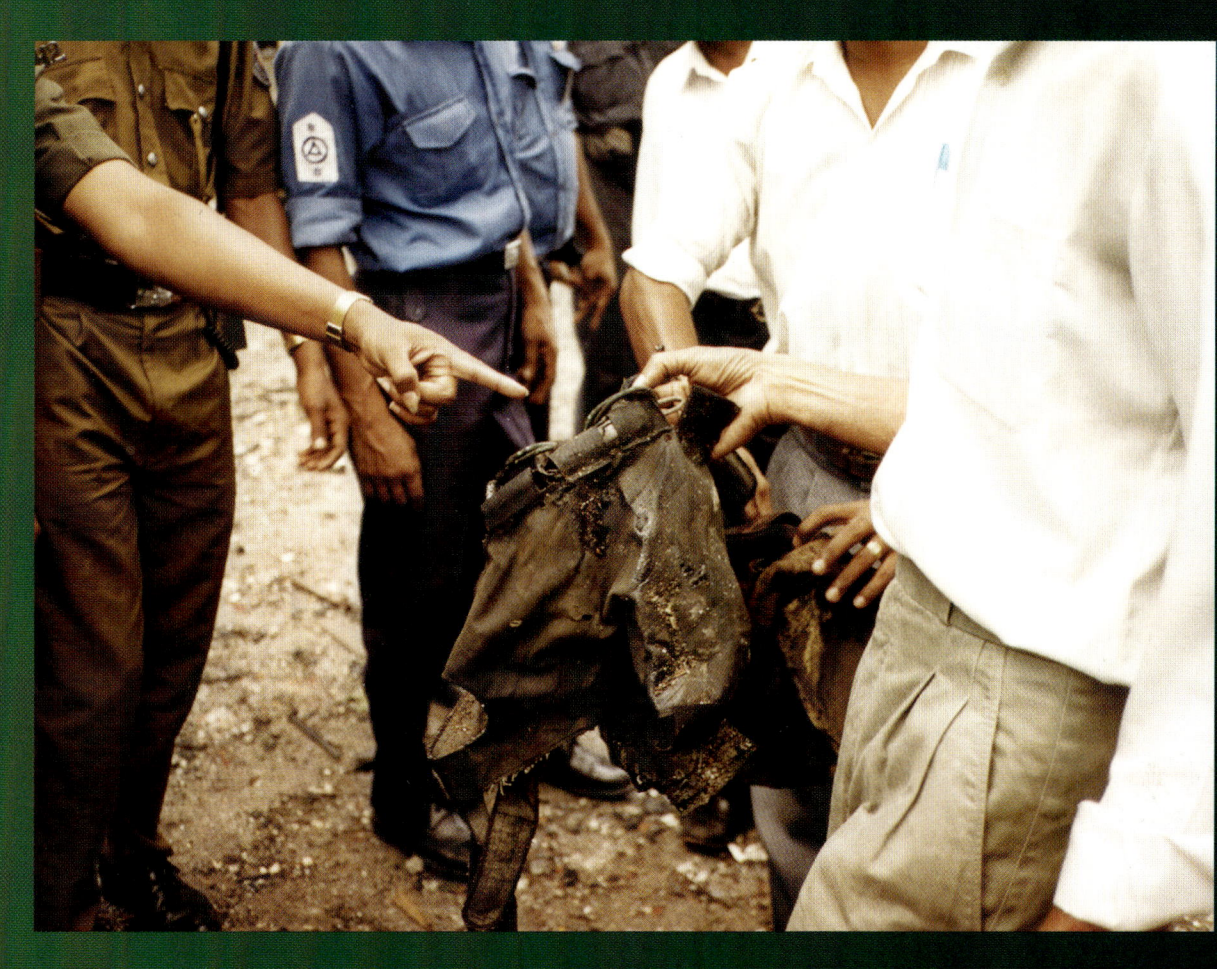

A rare picture of an unexploded LTTE suicide jacket. This one was discarded by one of the Central Bank bombers and hung on railings beside the Ceylinco Building just across the road. Explosives and electronics were still intact within the pockets. I saw it hanging on the railings and drew it to the attention of the security forces. The LTTE are recognised in the intelligence community as world leaders in the development of suicide bomb technology, which they pioneered long before other terrorist groups. Indeed, there is some evidence that they sold on or traded their mastery of this grisly profession to other groups like Hamas and Hizbollah. *January 1996.*

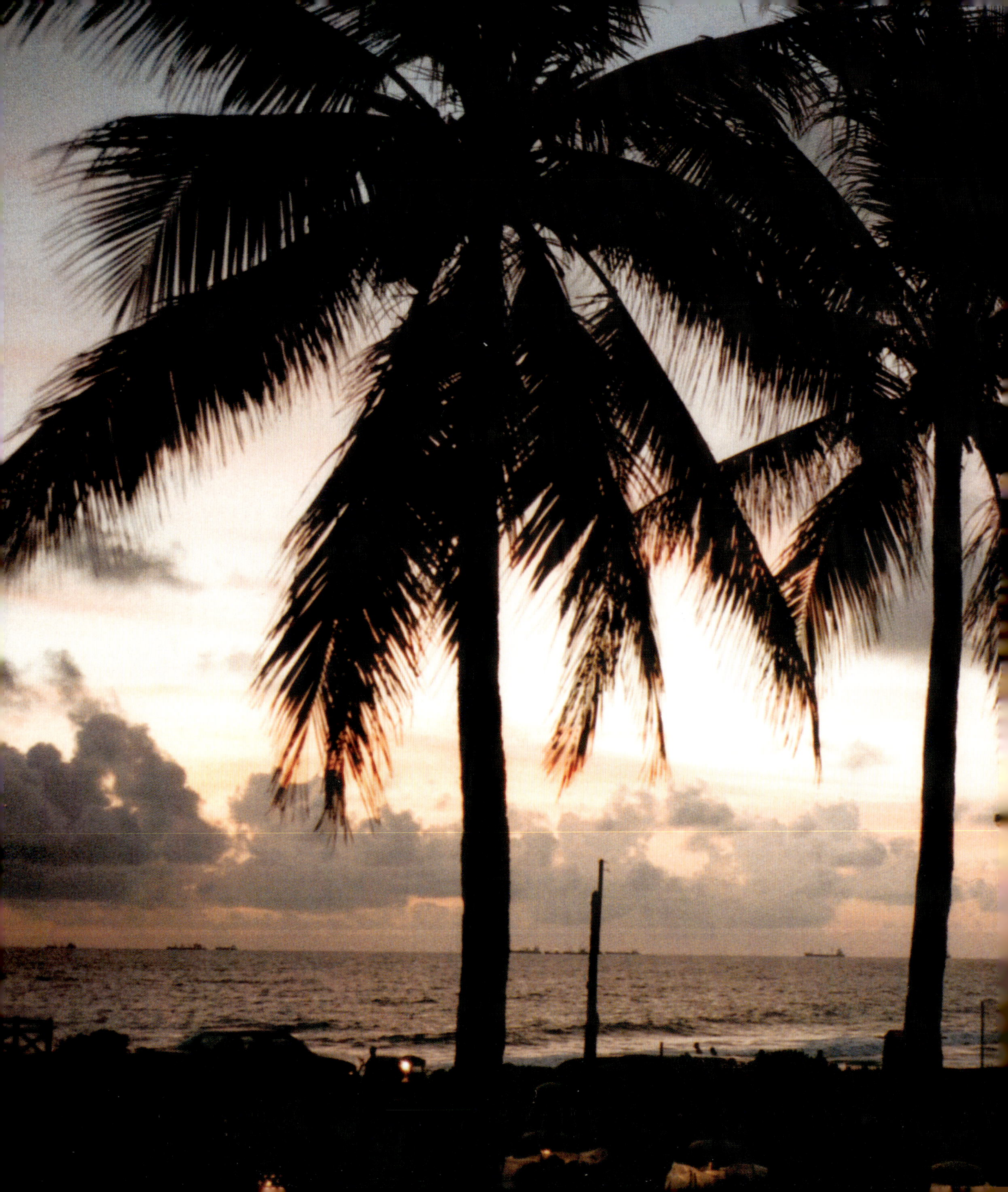

The view from the
terrace of the
Galle Face Hotel
as the sun goes down
can be breathtaking.
A cool beer at
sunset is the high point
of many a day in
Colombo.

October 2000.

The Galle Face Hotel. Colombo's most charming hotel was founded in 1864 and is known to its afficionados simply as 'the GFH'.
The letterhead boasts 'Yesterday's charm and tomorrow's comfort'. Facilities may not exactly be five-star, but for those seeking a genuine flavour of old Ceylon you can't beat the ageing splendour of the GFH with its teak floors, antique furniture and liveried servants.
October 2000.

Doorman at the Galle Face Hotel, K C Kuttan - 'Chattu' - has worked at the 'GFH' for an incredible 58 years. He joined at the age of 19 back in 1942. Many of the employees have completed more than 50 years of service, some having joined as young as 12 years old. Rather more of a gentleman than many of the guests these days, Chattu says fondly, "There was a time when all the high people who visited came here to stay. This was place was Number One. Now there are many hotels . . . ". *February 1999.*

The dream of yesterday and the reality of today. Red pillarbox dating from the days of the British Empire and the poverty of a present day street dweller in the Pettah district. *April 1996.*

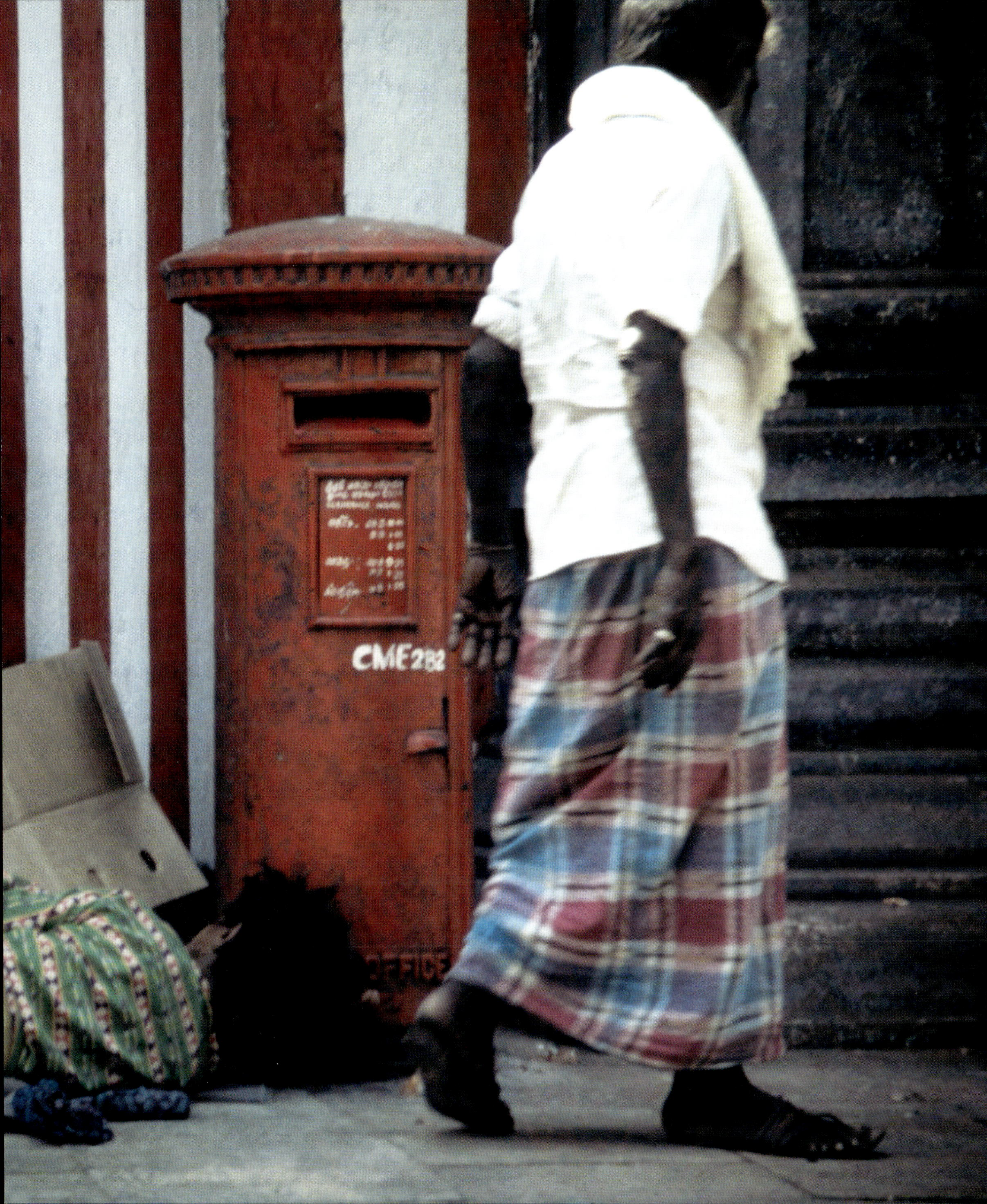
CME282

A good natured protest by workers outside the Galle Face Hotel. They protested over their remuneration during their own lunch breaks and then returned to work. *June 1996.*

Jaffna

My first approach to Sri Lanka's war ravaged northern peninsula of Jaffna in the spring of 1996 was inauspicious.

The twenty-five year old Avro passenger aircraft banked steeply and dropped to just fifty feet above the clear blue of the Indian Ocean passing between four anchored navy ships marking a 'safe' channel. Above us two Vietnam-vintage Bell Huey helicopters flew top cover, gunners visible, pilots firing orange flares which arced brilliantly over the ocean trailing white smoke before they dropped and were extinguished. The pyrotechnics aren't for show. They are to deter heat-seeking missiles. Out of the window I can see the polished metal plate affixed to the engine housing aft of the propellor - Rolls Royce it proclaims. This little bit of familiarity is reassuring. This is the Sri Lanka Air Force's last Avro. The other two have been shot down by Tamil Tiger rebels on this regular run from the capital Colombo into Jaffna's Palaly air base.

On the ground, the evidence could be seen of transport aircraft flying in and out of Palaly A diverse range of supplies were piled at the edge of the runway: ammunition, medical supplies, sacks of potatoes and, even, insulated containers of ice cream. Antonov AN-24 planes, flown by Kazakhi pilots, were flying soldiers in on a shuttle service, four aircraft at a time for security, with helicopters flying top cover. The Sri Lankan air force's key offensive assets - three Ukrainian Mi-24 helicopter gunships armed with heavy machine guns and rockets - could be seen refuelling and re-arming at the edge of the air base before returning to the battle which was going on to the south for the control of the strategic town of Kilinochchi. Soldiers, flying in 100 at a time, and including elite commandos in their red berets, relaxed on the grass at the side of the runway, their kit and weapons spread out beside them, waiting for the command to move off.

As the tide of war has ebbed and flowed, Jaffna and its city has always been the heartland of the Liberation Tigers of Tamil Eelam, their psychological home. In October 1995, the Sri Lankan army launched a massive offensive in a bid to take that heartland. Militarily, it seemed impossible. Materiel and 70,000 men all had to be flown into a narrow strip of land around Palaly air base: all that was then left of government held territory in the peninsular. As the military machine rolled out, taking territory in the wake of artillery bombardment, the Tigers forced virtually the entire population to leave their homes in an exodus to refugee status. And so, 900,000 people flooded out of Jaffna with whatever they could carry or load onto carts.

Then, in just six weeks, more than 400,000 Tamils chose to return. On the hot dusty road from Palaly to Jaffna city there was ample evidence of people returning home in old cars, trishaws, buffalo carts and on foot. White flags at the gates of houses set back from the road announce that the owners have returned home. Jaffna University reopened its doors and around 900 of the 3,000 students returned. All the computers and expensive equipment in science, medecine and agriculture departments was plundered by the retreating rebels, according to Vice Chancellor Professor Balasunderampillai.

At one of the largest girls' school - Jaffna Hindu Ladies' College - the story is similar. Around 40% of the girls have returned to their studies. Incredibly, every one of the three hundred or so girls who are gathered in the assembly hall are turned out in pristine white uniforms, striped ties and hair in neat pigtails. They describe how they have returned within the last four weeks from refugee camps. There is no running water or electricity in Jaffna and their turnout clearly reflects an extraordinary determination to return to normality.

In Jaffna City - a ghost town a few weeks previously - businesses were reopening and people crowded the roads. On the pavement a man with an aged manual typewriter knocked out letters for a few rupees a time. A private school

35

advertised English lessons. A shell damaged optician's shop was open again, although there was no sign of any customers. People on the streets complained about high prices, about the blackmarket and a shortage of food but they appeared to be grateful, like harried victims of war anywhere, for peace and the opportunity to return home.

Military presence was everywhere: sharpshooters atop the damaged buildings, foot patrols moving warily about, and South African-built Buffel armoured cars touring the streets. But what was truly surprising to me is the cordiality evident in relations between the military and the people. There is much handshaking, geniality and banter. People have no complaints about the soldiers but they will not be drawn on the Tigers.

I wrote these thoughts at the time. 'Here is a window of opportunity for the government in Colombo. If food, services and infrastructure can be layered on top of the opportunity provided by the military then this could turn out to be a textbook classic. There are very few examples in recent history of government forces beating a group of rebel insurrectionists on the battlefield and then winning the hearts and minds of the people on the ground. The opportunity is there in Jaffna.

On the other hand, it could all too easily turn out to be a terrible disaster. It wouldn't take too many incidents to alienate the population. At Point Pedro Hospital there are three women in one of the wards. A mother, in her mid-thirties, her 16 year-old daughter and her aunt. The mother is demented. The daughter, poignant beyond belief, bears a perpetually puzzled expression. This is the unmistakable look of a woman who has suffered some terrible, catastrophic wrong. Jaffna, Bosnia, Rwanda. The look is the same.

The men in uniform came to the door at night. A relatively well to do family, trading in addictive betel leaves, they had gold hidden in the house. Which is probably why, unlike their neighbours, they hung on. On the night of May 19 their house was effectively in No Man's Land between Tigers and army. Their gold was discovered, the women taken outside beaten, raped, genitally mutilated and branded on their foreheads. The LTTE in London announced the women were dead - killed by the army. The army says this disinformation proves the Tigers did this. Army, Tigers or freelances it is academic.

It is the fate of ordinary people like this will now determine the battle for hearts and minds in Jaffna.

Almost five years later, little seemed to have changed upon return to Jaffna. Traders and civilian population both relied upon insecure and extended links with the the southern part of the island. For goods, and most civilians, the link was either the sea route from Trinco into the port of Kankesanturai, or offshore unloading at Point Pedro. Although the Red Cross had succeeded in getting immunity from attack for the passenger vessel City of Trincomalee, the route was unreliable and insufficient to carry the vast number of people who wished to travel. The government offensive to open up the land route - Operation Jaya Sikuru - had not been assured of the certain victory which its nomenclature in Sinhalese had so optimistically promised.

Passenger flights for civilians in and out of Pallaly had come to an end after the downing of a passenger aircraft off the north east coast. Nobody professed to know whether it was down to mechanical failure or SAM shootdown. And the operating company Lionair was wound up shortly afterwards. The isolation was almost complete.

Much of Jaffna still lay in ruins. The unrepaired ruins of buildings like the Jaffna Library, the Post Office and the fort spoke volumes of man's destructive capability recently revisited upon once proud and elegant structures.

Politics and life carried on amidst the ruins. The man who emerged as kingmaker in the October 2000 elections, Douglas Devenanda, was a charismatic if shadowy figure. His supporters were armed by the authorities and acted both as political activists and, distrubingly, as an unofficial militia in the Jaffna Peninsular. These days, Devenanda opposes the LTTE but some people allege this was not always the case. His Eelam People's Democratic Party (EPDP) joined democratic politics in 1987 but prior to this had operated as a subversive militant group. In the late '80s, Devenanda returned from exile in India and formed the EPDP with government help. He is now not only the most powerful politician in Jaffna but in October 2000 became the key to the future of the government in Colombo.

Jaffna. Sri Lanka government forces retook the Jaffna Peninsular in December 1995. *July 1996*

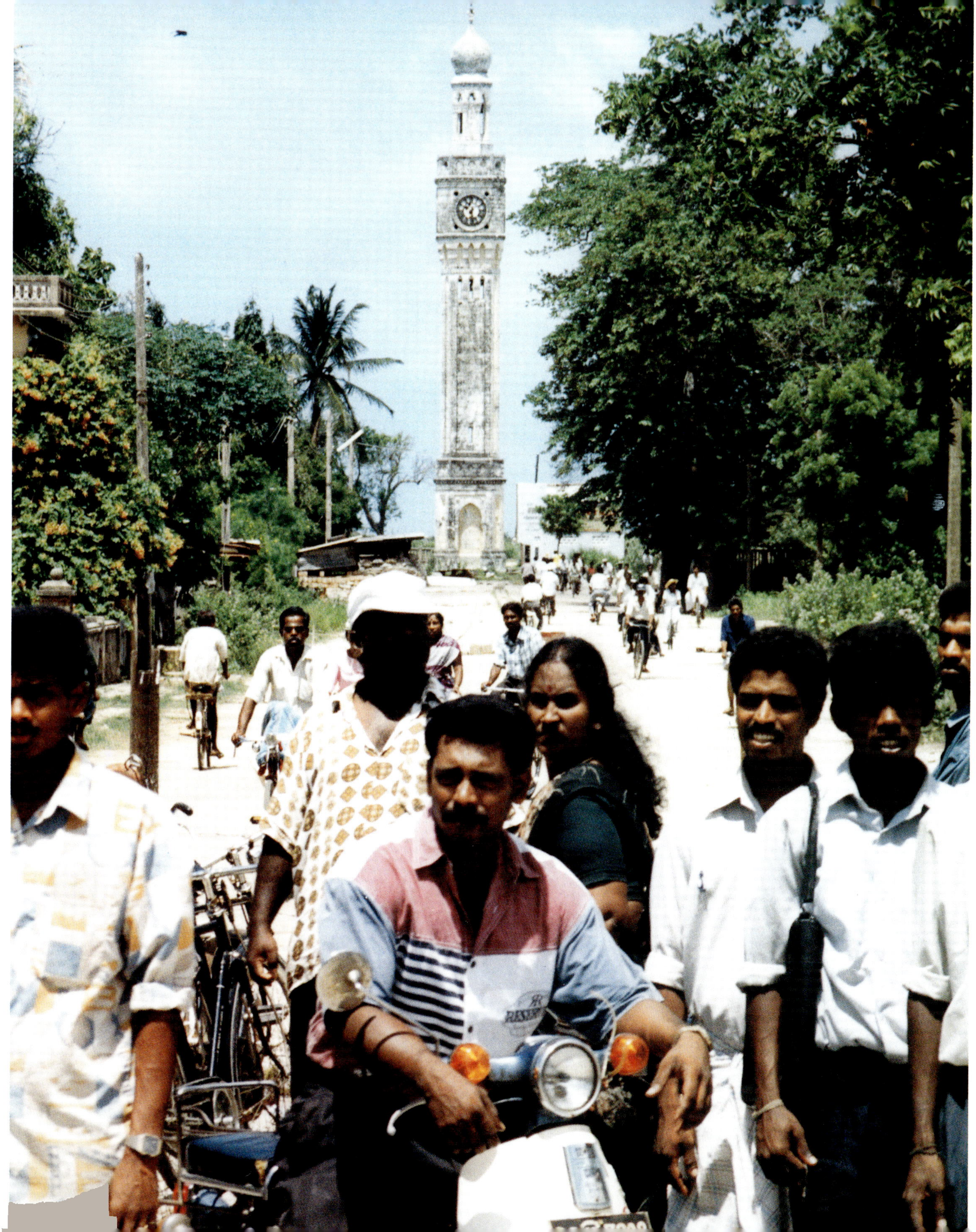

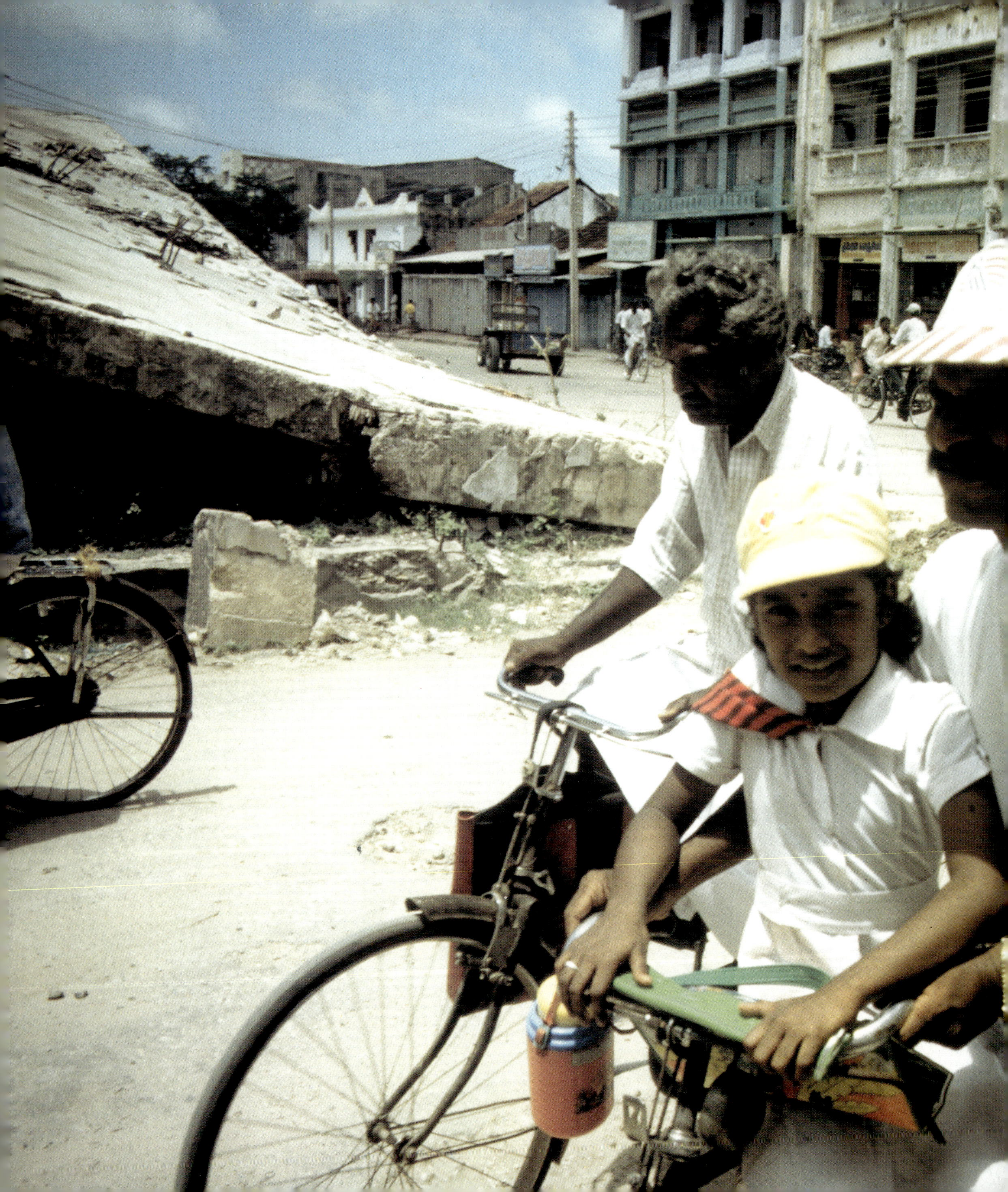

Near to the bus station in the centre of Jaffna.

Despite the widespread destruction caused by more than fifteen years of war, it is remarkable how life carries on in the beleagured Jaffna Peninsular: people carry on with their work as best they can and smartly-dressed children make their way to school and college. *June 1996.*

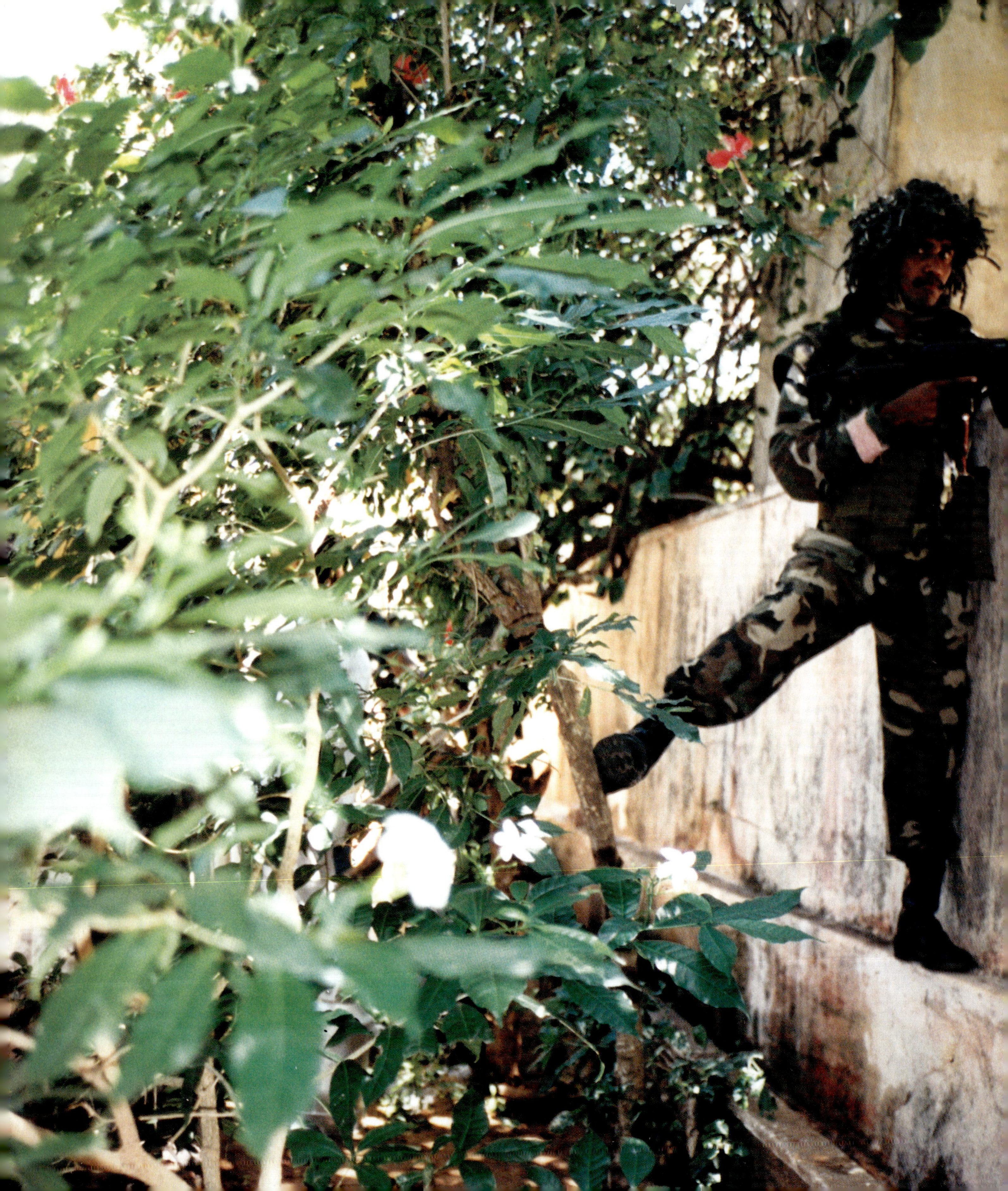

Time warp. The citizens of Jaffna keep an extraordinary number of old British cars dating from the 1950s on the road. This Austin A40 would now be a collector's item back in Britain, its country of origin. Restrictions on communications with the rest of Sri Lanka, with the Tamil Tigers occupying the Wanni region to the south, mean that only the most essential goods are brought in by ship to either Point Pedro or Kankesanthurai. Cars are not on any priority list and so people in Jaffna are obliged to keep their old vehicles in working order. *February 1999.*

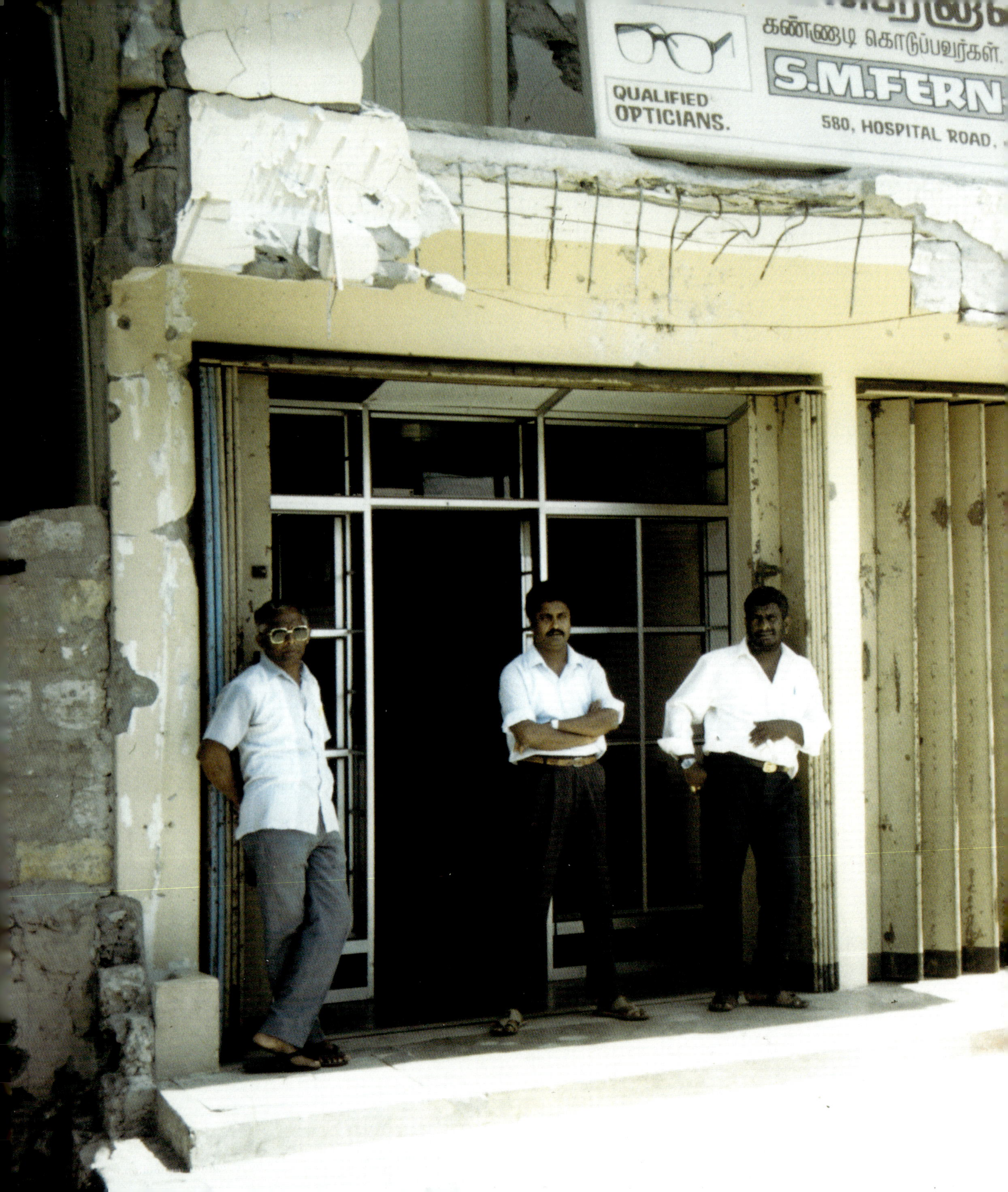
கண்ணாடி கொடுப்பவர்கள்.
QUALIFIED OPTICIANS.

In the shadow of the gun. Those parts of the Jaffna Peninsular under government control are secured by around 35,000 members of the security forces. Without such a heavy police and military presence the LTTE would quickly overrun the entire peninsular. Whilst this presence protects the civilian population, it is also an overbearing influence which makes living in Jaffna tense and tedious with continual checkpoints, security precautions and the ubiquitous men and women in uniform. Some local people say it is more like living in a vast prison camp. *July 1996.*

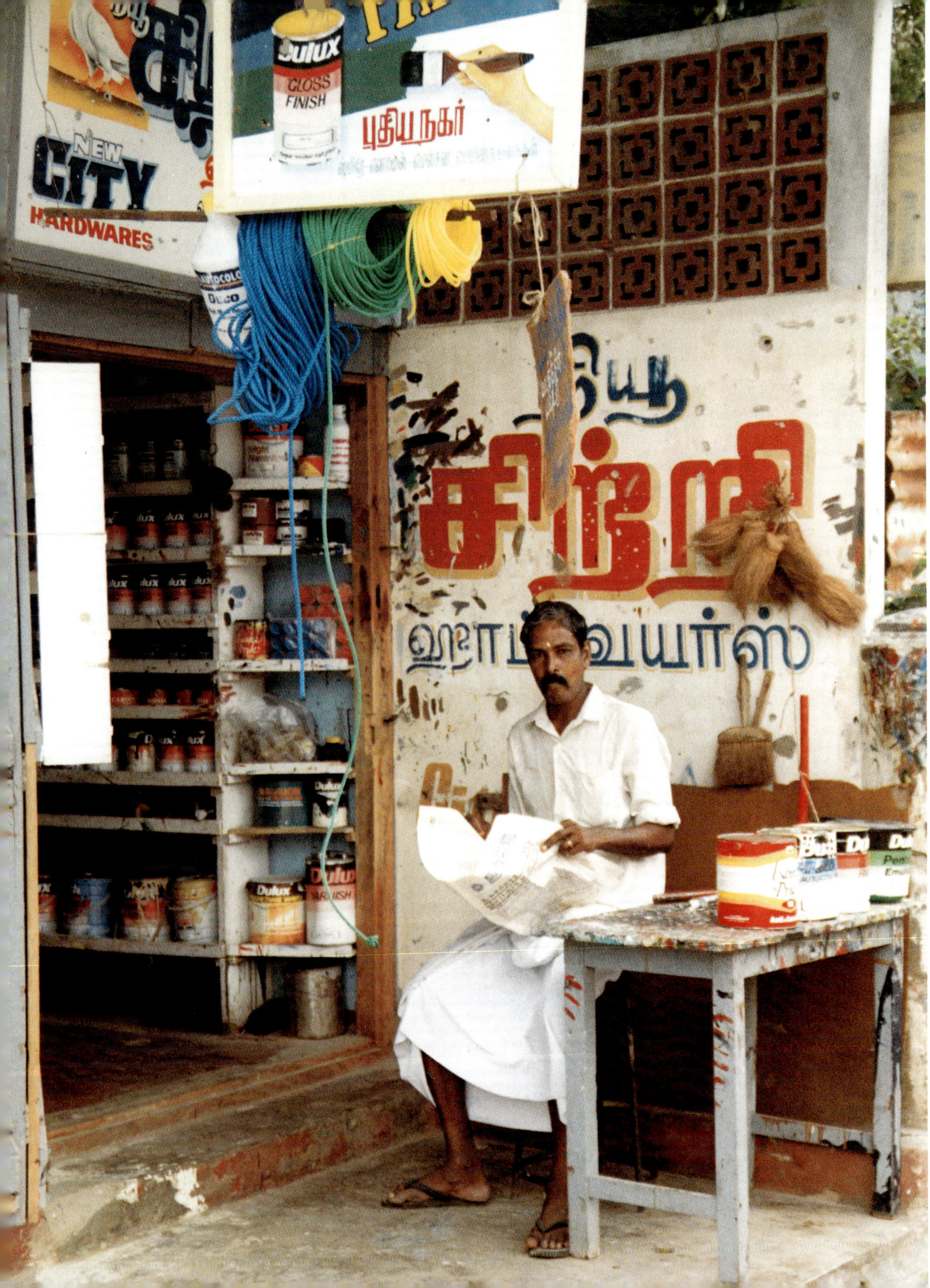
Dulux
GLOSS
FINISH
புதியநகர்
NEW
CITY
HARDWARES
Dulux

Under the difficult siege conditions prevailing in Jaffna town it is truly remarkable that any sort of business can be transacted. However, local businessmen seem enormously resilient. They seem to spend more time actually waiting for customers than serving them but there is always something for sale, albeit at higher prices than in Colombo. Many of the retail outlets still boast faded historic interiors of great charm. *July 1996 and October 2000.*

JAFFNA HINDU LADIES' COLLEGE
JAFFNA

Hearts and minds. Brigadier Sarath Munasinghe chats with students at Jaffna Hindu Ladies' College. He has since retired, entered politics and become Deputy Speaker in Parliment. *June 1996.*

Unsure. A young schoolgirl from St Mary's pictured in Hospital Road, Jaffna. *July 1996.*

On guard. Eternal vigilance is the key to survival for young soldiers working in Jaffna. They never know from where a threat might come. LTTE cadres mix with the local population - swimming like fish in the sea, to coin a phrase from Chairman Mao. *June 1996.*

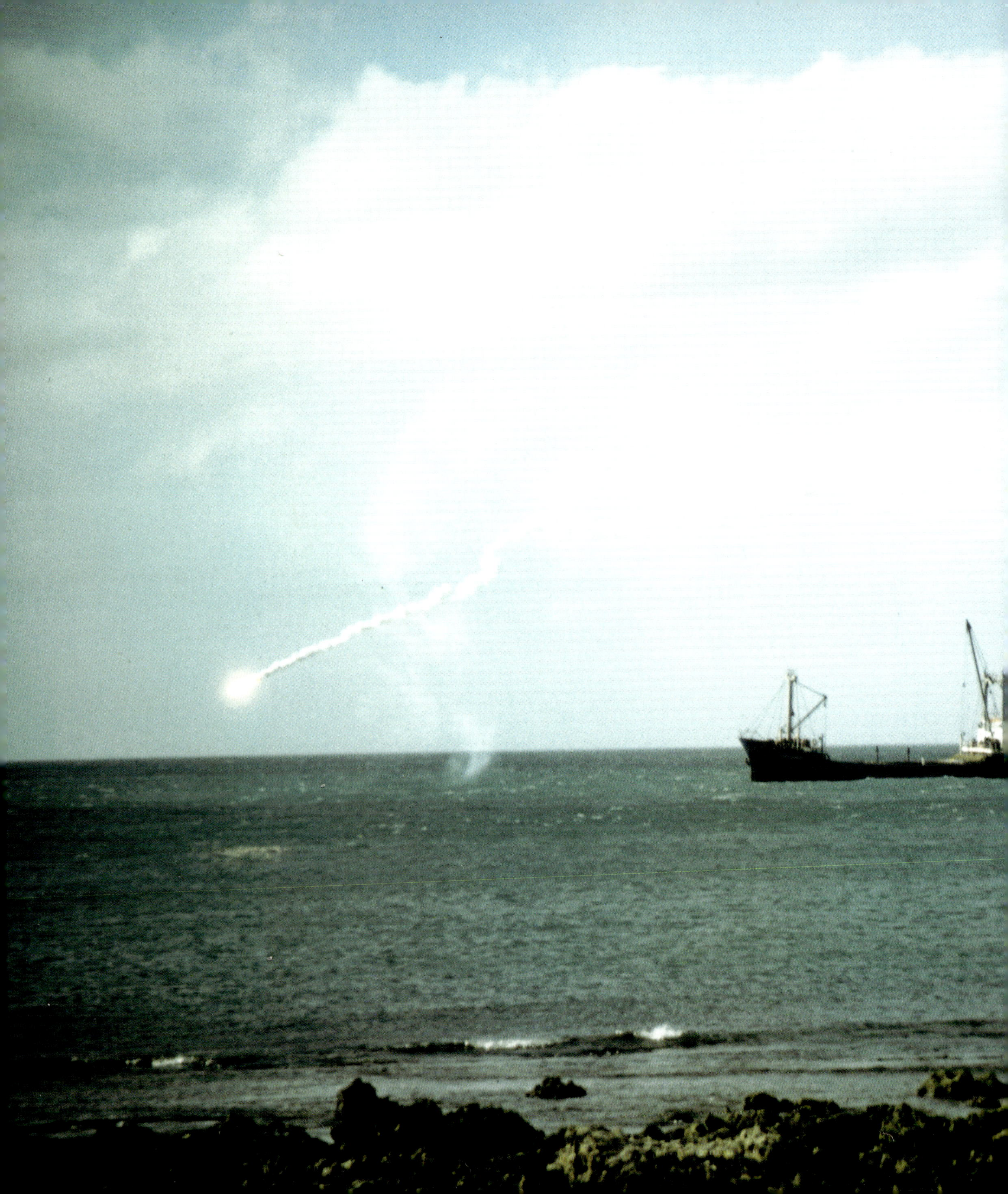

A Bell Huey military helicopter coming in to land at Point Pedro puts out flares to deter attack from heat-seeking surface to air missiles. *June 1996.*

Postcard from Jaffna. Ruins of the Jaffna Post Office, destroyed in fighting over the city. *July 1996.*

Group photograph. Sri Lanka Army (SLA) soldiers relax on the outskirts of Jaffna town. *June 1996.*

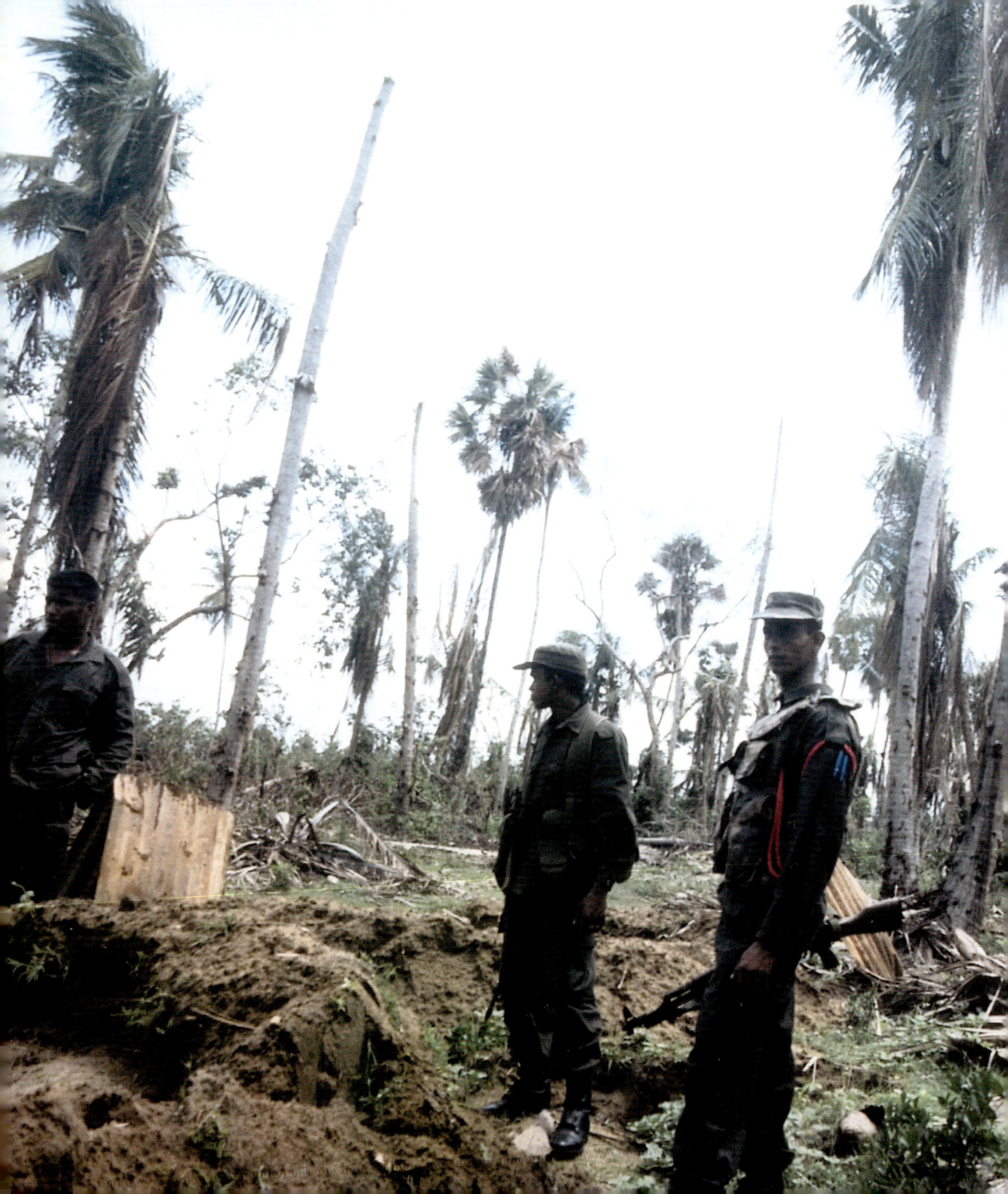

After the battle. Jungle devastation around an LTTE mortar position at Columbuthurai, south of the town of Jaffna, shortly after it was recaptured by the SLA. *October 2000.*

Graffiti military style celebrating the recapture of Columbuthurai. *October 2000.*

Escort vehicle on the outskirts of Jaffna town. *June 1996.*

Overleaf: The dove of peace flies above the United Peace Tower in the centre of Trincomalee. Trinco, as it is known, is home to what Admiral Lord Nelson termed "the finest natural harbour in the world" and is still of great strategic and, potentially, commercial importance. As such it is a prime target for the LTTE. *February 1999.*

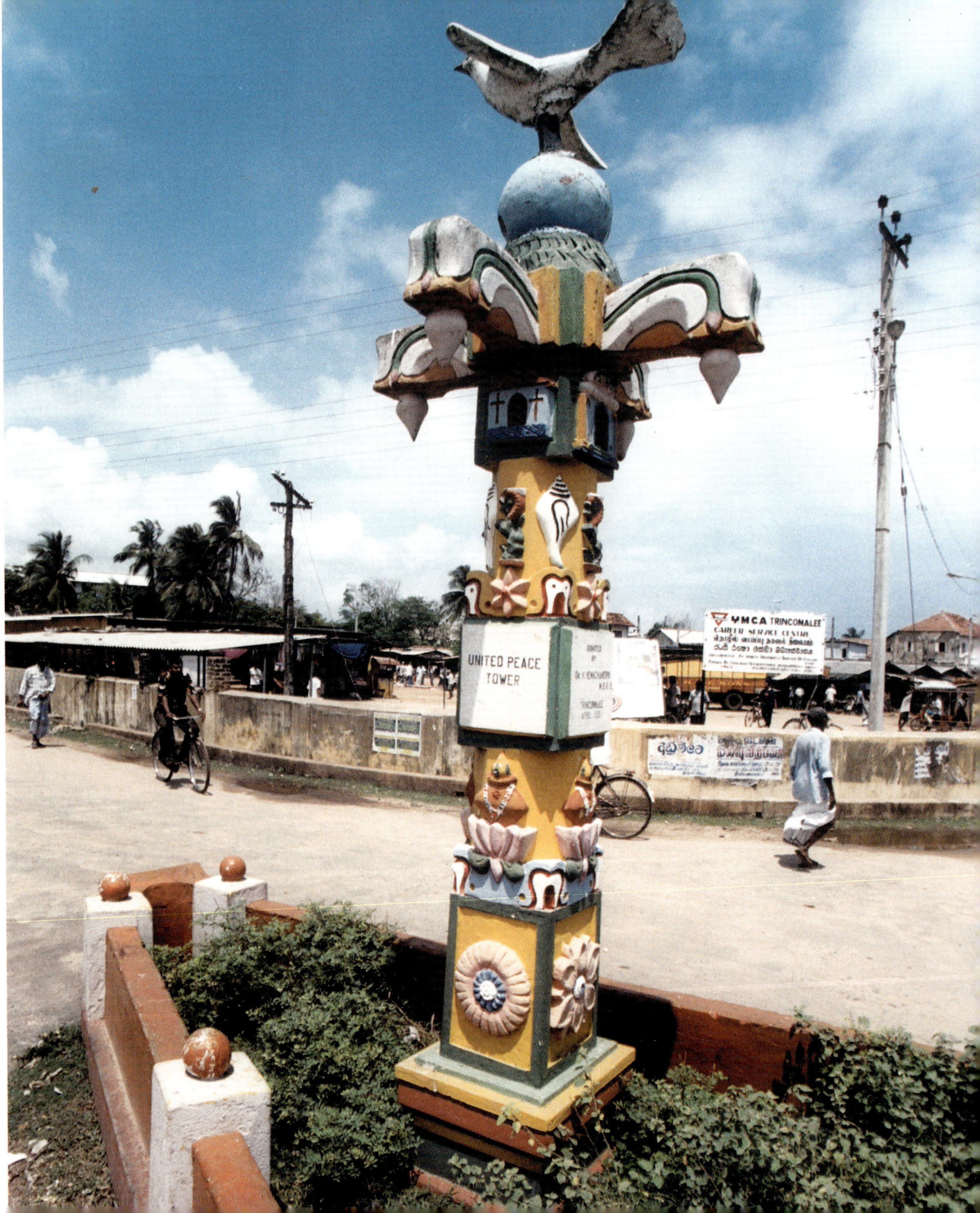
UNITED PEACE
TOWER
YMCA TRINCOMALEE

Batti & Trinco

This must surely be the thing to paradise.

If such a thing might exist on this earth. The turquoise blue waters of the Indian Ocean ripple gently onto pure white, palm-fringed sands which seemingly stretch away into infinity. My cool, air-conditioned hotel room opens directly onto the beach and, of a morning, it is an effortless 100 metre sprint into the clear, warm waters of the ocean. For the snorkeler, just beyond the gentle surf there are stunning, white coral reefs and shoals of exotic tropical fish. A couple of miles offshore over the clear water is Pigeon Island, breeding ground for the Blue Rock Pigeon. It is said Admiral Lord Nelson used the island for gunnery practice.

Over a breakfast of fresh pineapple it is already time to consider dinner. Yes, lobster, would be fine and a boatman is engaged to catch your dinner. Here, there's no pollution, no sewage. No hawkers on the beach - well, there is one inoffensive chap on a bicycle selling spectacular conches at a couple of dollars a go. No deafening disco. No drunken louts. No noise of jet skis. No film of suntan oil on the clear, still waters of the swimming pool. As the sun sets over the Indian Ocean and the blue sea turns a reddish grey you tuck into prefectly prepared lobster, sweeter and fleshier than it seemed possible to imagine.

Members of staff busy themselves catering for your every need. This all sounds so perfect that you might rightly wonder why when I tell you that sometimes I have been the only guest in the Nilaveli Beach Hotel. That paradise remains beyond the reach of all but a very few. Rightly, it should be at the top of the list of Asia's dream hotels.

Manager Mr V Prem Kumar told me back in 1997 that, most of the time, he just sat in the hotel alone with 20 members of staff. For the 23 year-old Nilaveli Beach Hotel was, and still is, on the front line in Sri Lanka's war: it effectively exists as an oasis of luxury and safety in the no man's land of war. It is, indeed, a strange, bizarre haven and its continued existence is something of a mystery even to those who are in on the secret.

In the early 1980s, tourist hotels mushroomed along the north east coast of Sri Lanka in the area north of the port of Trincomalee, 'Trinco' as it is known, dubbed 'the best natural harbour in the world' by Nelson. The vast white beaches and the warm, blue waters combined with mean temperatures around 28 degrees made it perfect for tourist development. The science fiction writer Arthur C Clarke, from his base in the Sri Lankan capital of Colombo, bought land for a deep sea diving school and investors poured into the area. Until the summer of 1985 the hotels on the east coast were full with western tourists but, that year, the tentacles of war spread - and the tourists stayed away.

Most of the Colombo-based owners abandoned their hotels to looting and decay: just next door the Blue Lagoon hotel lies deserted and ruined. Others that attempted to stay in business were destroyed. That summer the Moonlight Hotel, just a couple of hundred metres the other side of the Nilaveli Beach Hotel, was blown up by the LTTE. Its eerie, collapsed ruins and its stagnant, sludge filled swimming pool stand in silent testimony to what happens to a tourist industry when war arrives.

Somehow Nilaveli has stubbornly remained in business - with virtually no business to speak of - as the war has ranged around it. The barman reminisces about the summer of 1985 when there were almost three hundred guests packed into the 90 rooms laid out in whitewashed, terraced bungalows. A photograph of a throng of extravagantly uniformed and sarong-clad staff at the opening in 1974 hangs in the office does show that things are not quite as they were. Nevertheless, as the tropical dawn breaks at 7 a.m., workers are already busying themselves scooping overnight fallen leaves from the pool, brushing the tennis court, polishing the tiled floor of the open-sided restaurant, sandpapering and varnishing its columns of coconut timber, sweeping the paths which wind through the low fruit mand beech trees connecting the bungalows to the main block - they are even sweeping the beach to smooth the sand for the visitors who may, or may not, come. Royalty could hardly fare better. But, as you make your way up the narrow, broken road to Nilaveli, past a series of rigorous army checkpoints and through the heavy iron gates set in a high wall, the place is an enigma.

The engaging Mr Kumar is, first and foremost, a professional hotelier who professes to enjoy his work. He also seems to be a bit of a philosopher, which must be a prerequisite in his position. Born in Jaffna, in the Tamil heartland in the north of the country, he's married to a Christian. "Same roof, different houses but the roof always safeguards you when it rains. " He believes that men should live in peace. That in this limited time on earth we should behave to each other as brothers. That it is the politicians who cause problems in the pursuit of power.

Yes, but how does this hotel survive when all around are destroyed; in an area where the military abandon any attempt to control the roads after nightfall and the LTTE control supreme; where residents of the nearby Moslem village of Iqbal Nagar fled their homes eighteen months ago, when the LTTE attacked the police post ? They elected to take everything with them, including roofs and window frames, never to return.

"Well, you see, this hotel is running in a neutral way. We are not interested in politics. We just do hotel business." The holding company - Mercantile Investments Ltd - has other interests in hotels and tourism but they can hardly be subsidising Nilaveli: tourism is at an all time low after dramatic, high profile terrorist attacks. Mr Kumar shrugs his shoulders, "We have a few guests. We survive." The reflection of the floodlights and fairylights twinkle in the waters of the pool ($300 a month to maintain) and, just beyond, arc lights illuminate the entire beach frontage for hundreds of yards in both directions.

As we talk on the terrace as the sun slips down, there is a long, deep rumbling sound. Mr Kumar looks pained.

I forebear to comment. Then it is repeated. We both know what this is. It is the sound of heavy artillery fire.

Says Sri Lank'a most resilient hotelier, "It is a very long way away, maybe 50 miles. Don't worry." Sound travels far in the still of the tropical night. And he adds, "We will never give up. We will never lose hope. We will never close."

There's no road into the village of Kumbulijanpattimadu. Just a narrow, sandy track. Your feet sink into the sand and it's hard going, even though it's less than 400 yards from the main road. There's not much shade either. The army have burned the trees and scrub a hundred yards back from the road. For security, you see. Once you get just a couple of hundred yards from the main road in eastern Sri Lanka you're out of army controlled territory and into a sort of uneasy No Man's Land. By night, the Tamil Tigers rule here. Sometimes, even, by day as well.

The dull crump is most probably a long way away. Sound travels in the still, airless atmosphere. Somewhere down the road to the north somebody is shelling somebody. Who knows around here ? There are no front lines. Just a ribbon of road, a string of defended army positions, endless checkpoints and, for the military, an invisible enemy. They are terrorists to the army and the government, freedom fighters to the majority of the indigenous Tamil population around here.

All around, the coconut palms are stripped of their bounty. Local people say that the soldiers come and steal the coconuts to deny them food. The army says the terrorists take them. Who knows?

Parting the scrub where it overhangs the path, I get my first sight of the village. Or, rather, what is left of it. The houses of coconut palms on a wooden framework, fragile to start with, bear the clear evidence of some disaster. Most are holed or damaged in some way. The salvable dwellings are covered in blue plastic sheeting brought here by the NGOs. It may keep the monsoon rains out and hold the heat at night but, in the middle of the day, it makes the inside of the huts unbearably hot. Looking around, you see that many houses have disappeared completely. Of some, just four or six charred uprights remain, of others only the foundations.

The army came to Kumbulijanpattimadu on the night of November 19 1995. Nodody disputes that. The villagers tell how they fled before the gunfire and grenades and how, as they fled, they saw their village burning as it was put to the torch. The people at the ICRC and Medecins sans Frontieres confirm it. Even the army admits to it. You see, the terrorists were hiding here and attacking traffic on the road. Who knows?

Villages like this have become the battlegrounds in Sri Lanka's civil war. After government troops seized the centre of the traditional northern Tamil heartland of Jaffna in a massive offensive in October 1995, large numbers of the LTTE were displaced into the east of the island where an army weakened by its commitment to the battle in the north was pulling back and abandoning territory. By night, the Tamil Tiger guerillas hold all of it apart from the defended military bases and other government installations. By day, the soldiers emerge and attempt to secure a single eighty kilometre long road running from the crossing into Tiger territory at Welikande to the regional capital of Batticaloa, a small pretty town on the edge of a vast blue lagoon.

Excesses seem to be in the nature of bitter conflicts like this. The Tigers emerge and kill soldiers. Until recently that was just at night. Now they are bold enough to hit and run during the day. They are inflicting crippling casualties: a recent attack at one base - just a few miles from the village where I am now surveying a panorama of destruction - killed more than 70 soldiers in broad daylight. Then the military go in pursuit of their elusive foe. Sometimes they think they have found them. Sometimes they just get mad. And the villages burn.

I have been in Kumbulijanpattimadu for almost an hour when I realise it. There is something very strange indeed here. This village is full of children. There is not an adult male to be seen. Not a child older than about thirteen or fourteen. In the distance, scurrying between huts there are a couple of women both pregnant. Where are the adults ? The farmers and fishermen who used to live here. The kids shrug their shoulders. They have gone away. Away to work ? They stare uneasily into the sand, furrowing it with their bare feet.

The fact is that such villages now represent a fertile recruiting ground for men and boys to join the Tiger cadres. Even the girls are joining. Down the road in Batticaloa, there were two fifteen year-old girls in the central police headquarters caught smuggling explosives at a checkpoint.

Other people, apparently, just plain disappear around here. Some go off to join the Tigers without telling friends or family. Others are taken away - either by the army or the Tigers. It's been going on for years. In his top floor tower room in the crumbling Jesuit College in Batticaloa, 70 year-old Father Harry Miller shuffles through a pile of pink cards. They are his Event Cards. In 1990, he was so concerned at the abrogation of civil rights, at the disappearances and injustices - more people have disappeared in the last five years in Sri Lanka than in Nicaragua or El Salvador - that he set up a Peace Committee.

Bespectacled Father Miller, from New Orleans, knows the situation intimately. He's in with the decaying woodwork. He's been here since 1947 and commands universal respect : religious leader, enthusiastic Rotarian, founder of the Citzens' Committee and the Peace Committee, the Batticaloa branch of the Red Cross Society, the Sri Lanka Cancer Society and the Society for the prevention of TB. "So many people were going missing and their relatives could find nothing out so we said 'Come to us and we will search for you'.

SLA training ground, Batticaloa. *April 1996.*

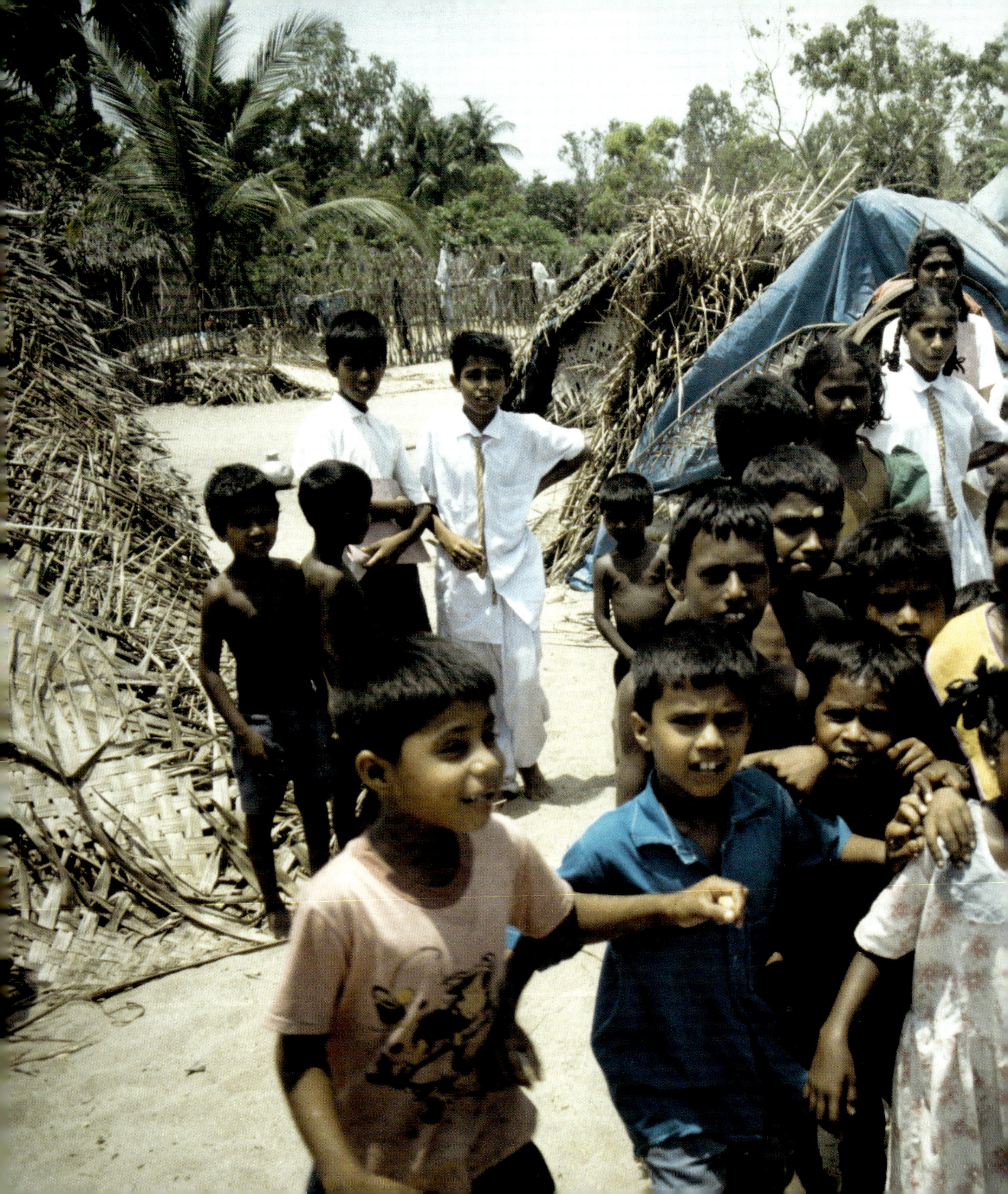

Children at the partially destroyed village of Kumbulijanpattimadu, just off the main road north of Batticaloa, live in tents fashioned from plastic sheeting and coconut palms. When I visited, there were no adults, apart from a couple of pregnant women, in evidence. Young boys, and some girls, are recruited into the LTTE at an early age. *April 1996.*

There is green, stagnant water in the abandoned swimming pool of the destroyed Midnight Hotel at Nilaveli. *February 1999.*

Opposite: The Nilaveli Beach Hotel somehow survives in the war zone north of Trincomalee.
A puzzling oasis of tranquillity, the war ebbs and flows around the grounds of the hotel but somehow rarely ever touches it. A kilometre offshore is Pigeon Island, a breeding ground for the Blue Rock Pigeon. In days of yore, Nelson used it for target practice. For the cognoscenti - and that includes myself - it is a weekend haven of peace despite the proximity of war.
February 1997.

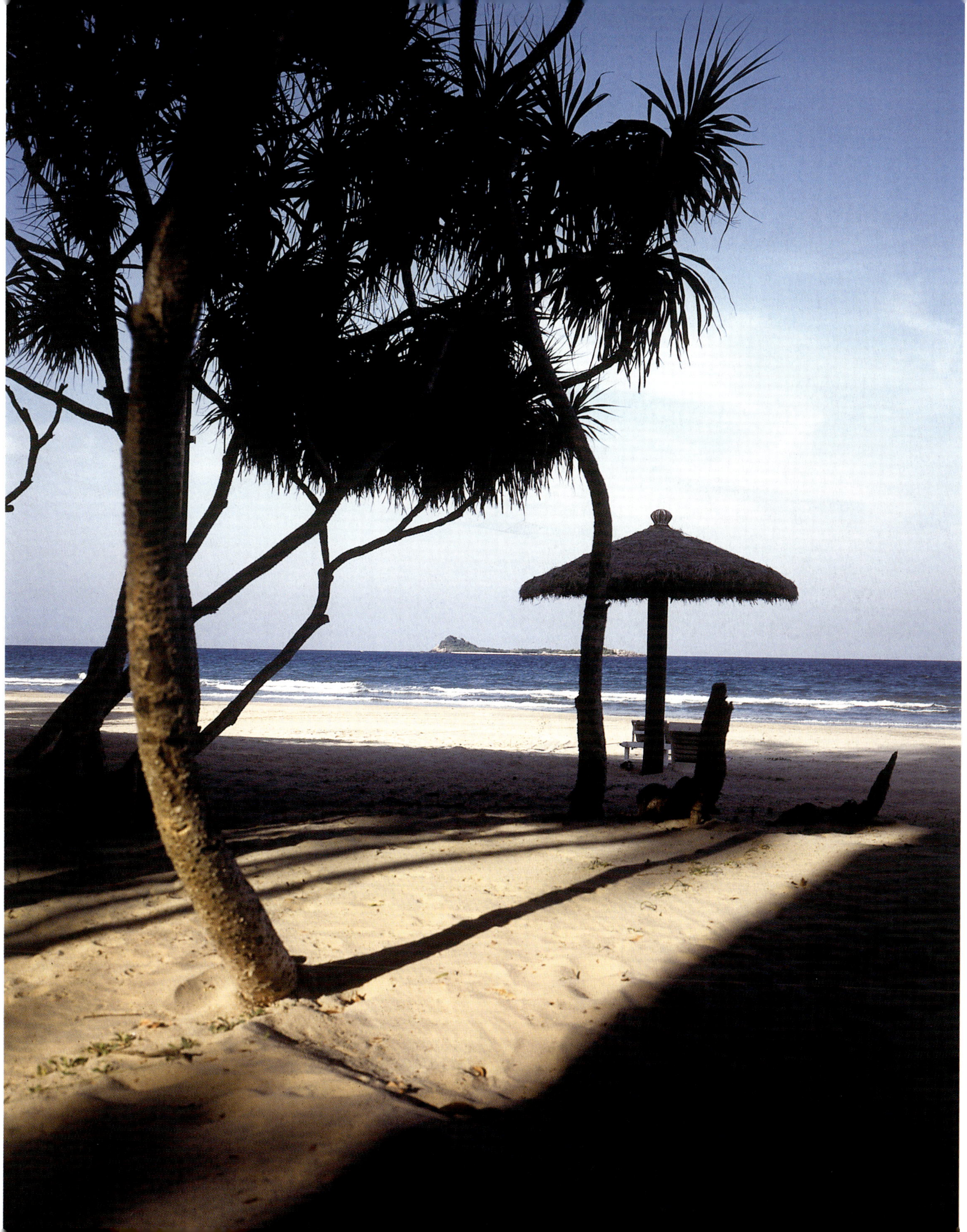

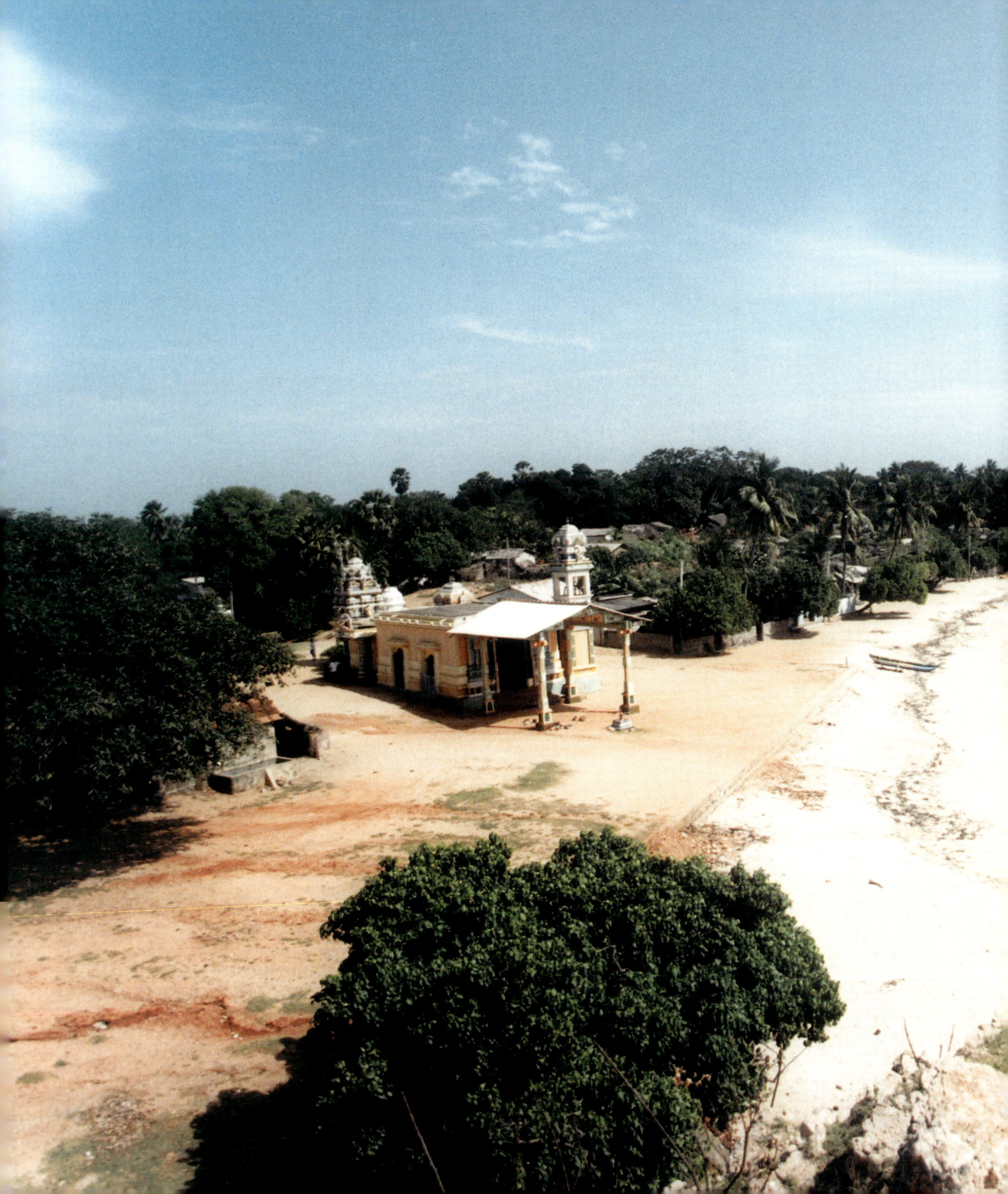

Temple on the beach at Sambaltivu, 10 km north of Trincomalee. The Salli Kovil, or Money Temple, is the site of an annual pilgrimage for Hindus who walk from Trinco. *February 1999.*

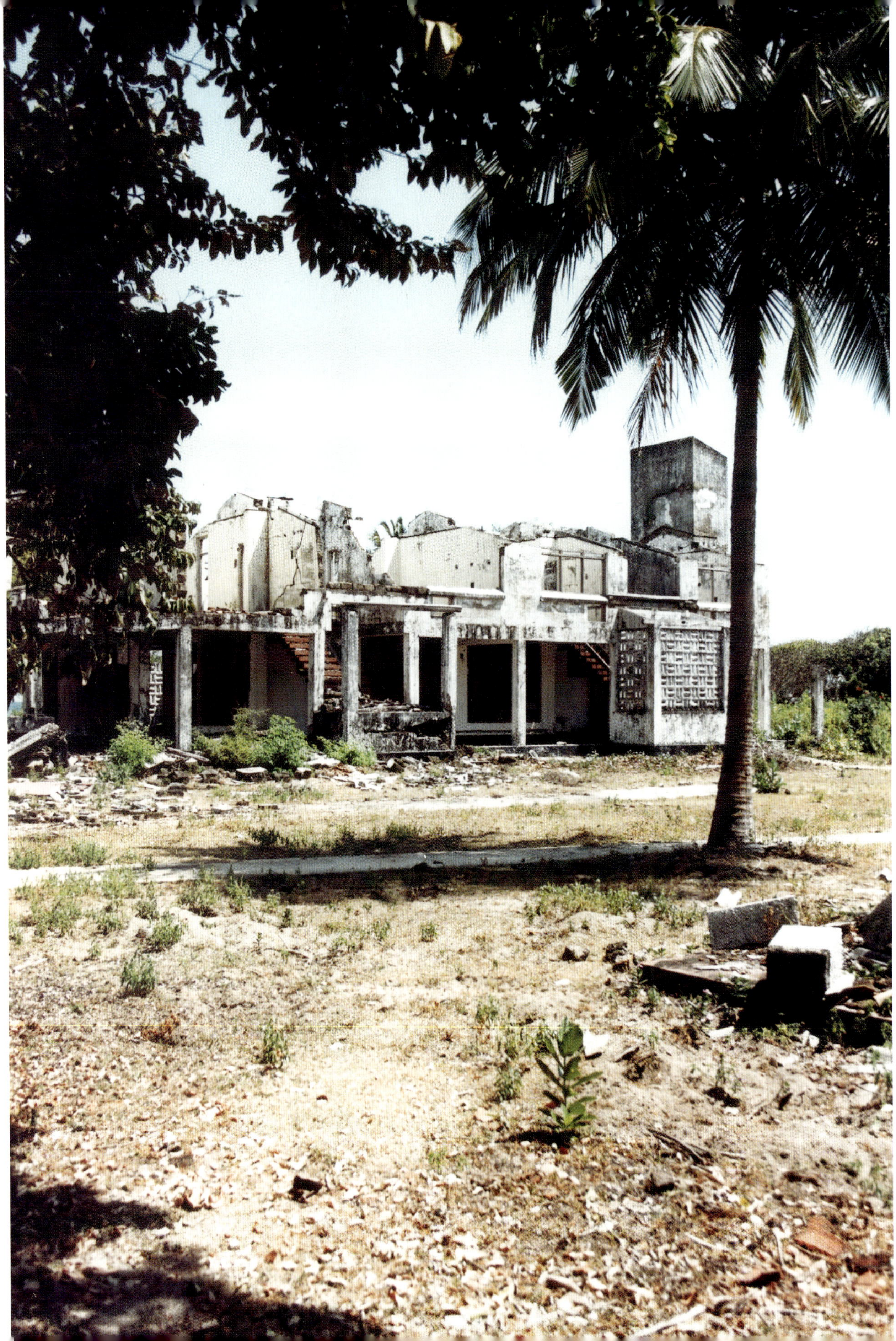

The causeway across the lagoon at Batticaloa. A location characterised by great tension, every person entering Batticaloa is systematically searched. Although the security forces control by day, once darkness falls the LTTE are in charge. *April 1996.*

Opposite: Ruins of the Midnight Hotel, Nilaveli. *February 1996.*

The Kanniyai Hot Springs near Trincomalee. Hindus come here to draw water from the seven wells. According to legend, the hot wells were created by Vishnu to distract the demon king Rawana who named them after his mother. These days they are under military protection. *February 1997.*

Opposite: Father Harry Miller, the Jesuit priest and passionate human rights advocate, who has worked tirelessly in Batticaloa for more than fifty years after arriving there from New Orleans. *April 1996.*

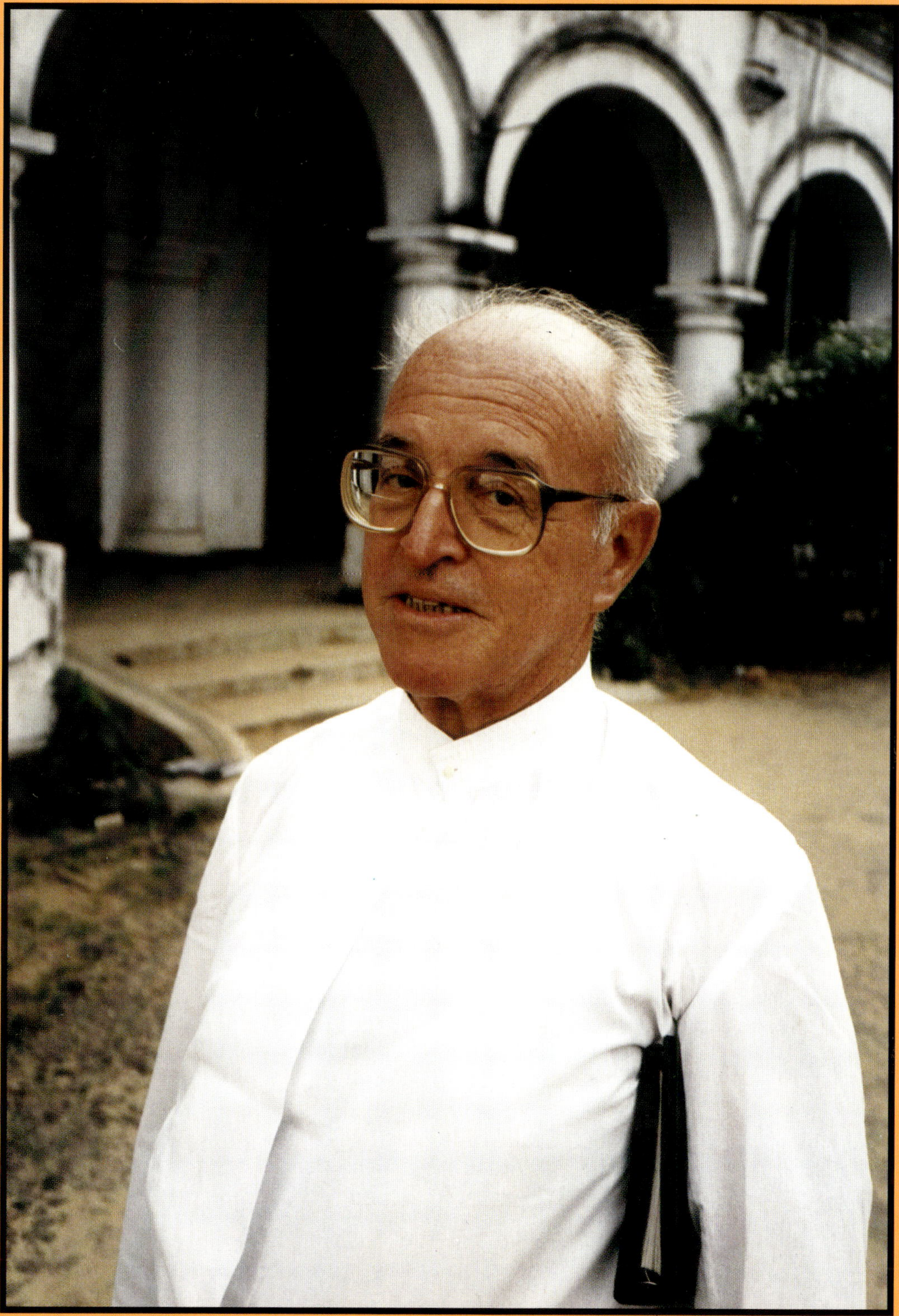

HRH The Prince of Wales shows off his gift of a cricket bat at the Sinhalese Sporting Club ground, Colombo. He continued with his official visit to Sri Lanka despite the bombing of the Dalada Maligawa in Kandy two weeks before his arrival. The British authorities secretly struck a hands-off deal with the LTTE in the Wanni jungle.
February 1998.

People

The last inhabitant of the Indian Ocean island of Sri Lanka to meet HRH The Prince of Wales on his state visit in February 1998 was a Sergeant Major in the Sri Lanka army.

Truth to tell, they didn't have much to say to each other. Before making his way up the steps to his aircraft, the Prince actually fed Sgt Maj Kandula, who was then four years in the army, bananas from a silver salver. This may sound like some anachronistic colonial charade straight from the movie set of *The Man Who Would Be King*, but needs must reveal that the bearer of this rank in the army was a small Ceylonese elephant. Sgt Maj Kandula enjoys his rank on the grounds of certain financial requirements for his feeding and maintenance.

His Colonel told me at the time, "If we didn't give him this rank we would not be able to draw down the money to keep him . . ." This was a bizarre mechanism to sidestep the former colony's multi-layered bureaucracy. That bureaucracy, such a tedious feature of British life, has been inherited here, preserved intact, embellished and developed to the status of a fine art. Indeed, everywhere there are relics of those colonial days: preserved with affection and curious lack of rancour.

British royalty is written of in the newspapers in the sort of reverential tones the British press last used around the time of the Coronation. In amongst the adverts for Lifebuoy toilet soap and Rinso washing powder, a correspondent reminisces fondly, if a trifle quaintly, "In the good ole days of British Colonial rule, we lived in peace, enjoying plenty of cheap bread and butter . . . the good ole days will never dawn again . . . [when] the Police Band was a must for all fashionable society functions and weddings and when the curtain fell they would play God Save the King".

When Charles shook hands and spoke with Arthur C Clarke at the State Banquet, the representatives of the British tabloid press went into a flat spin. Clarke was newly accused - on the basis of evidence dubiously acquired by a British tabloid newspaper whose representatives had entered the country illegally without press visas - of paedophilia. The correspondent of *The Sun* could be heard barking down his phone to copytakers in London, "Catchline Perv, Prince shakes hands with alleged sex pervert . . .". This sort of conduct is distasteful and mystifying to people in a former colonial country which adheres to the old values rather more rigorously than we do back in Britain - and we like to think we invented those values. As Fleet Street worked itself up into a flat spin, the Prince's 'dramatic' meeting with Arthur C Clarke did not receive one single column centimetre in any Sri Lankan newspaper the next day. . . one editor said he simply didn't regard it as newsworthy. By standards long forgotten in Britain that was probably a pretty fair assessment.

On the Thursday evening of his visit, the Prince made his way around the shady, treed garden at Westminster House, the British High Commissioner's large and opulent home in one of Colombo's poshest suburbs. Apart from the human relics of British colonialism, in their fading, shabby tropical whites, there were gathered the Sri Lankans who do business with Britain: the women glittering in their saris, their husbands cool and smooth in sober, dark suits. For these locals, the opportunity to meet Prince Charles was accepted graciously and with gratitude. There was undiluted admiration for his resolve to come to their country in the face of terrorist threats.

There are paradoxes everywhere: genial, ever-smiling locals and grim-faced troops; well preserved fifteen century-old architectural sites and bomb shattered buildings; quaint colonial comforts against the background of a modern war in paradise, and that tropical languor which can so suddenly turn to extraordinary violence. As you look at schoolboys playing cricket in their neatly pressed whites you cannot help but wonder at what point the crack of leather on willow will be replaced in their lives by the crackle of machine gun fire.

The island of Sri Lanka frequently gives the impression that very little has actually changed since the British left in fifty year ago in 1948. Some of the great institutions - like the army and the tourist office - still use Ceylon in their nomenclature. The army still uses British mess kit and customs, and bases its structure on the British army. This sunny disposition survives remarkably intact despite the exigencies of civil strife.

Temple Trees is what you might call a substantial colonial style residence. It is grand but not particularly ostentatious. Rather similar to the British High Commissioner's residence in many respects. On the lawn, which is dominated by a permanent satellite up-link dish placed there for the convenience of state television, an Indian journalist tells me a trifle disdainfully that it would be the home of a middle ranking member of parliament back in Delhi. The Indians, of course, feel a little superior when it comes to their small island neighbour. Sri Lanka may be inconsequential in terms of its diminutive size but it is on their exposed southern flank and it is regarded by New Delhi as coming firmly within their sphere of influence.

The most impressive features of Temple Trees are the complex and extensive defences which protect the personage of the President from the outrages of her fractious citizens: fencing, barricades, armed men and women from a bewildering range of security forces. There are body searches, x-rays and car ramp investigations. You can take cigarettes in but not lighters or matches, which presents nicotine addicts with something of a challenge. Truth to tell, the Presidential Security Division is still under something of a cloud. In December 1999, a Tamil Tiger woman suicide bomber penetrated security and blew herself up at a Presidential election meeting. The President was blinded in one eye by a small piece of shrapnel.

President Chandrika Kumaratunge is steely but not without charm. She is known locally as a 'streetfighter'; a scion of the distinctly upper-class Bandaranaike dynasty who gives as good as she gets in political fighting and is sometimes criticised in the press for her crude and vulgar language. Locals say she is not in the traditional mould of the Bandaranaikes. Of course, she was educated in Sri Lanka rather than in the ivory tower of an English public school where Ceylon's ruling elite were traditionally raised. She stands out as a genuine mix of old and new in a society where rulers, generals and ministers are often more English than the English.

Every now and then she reveals an endearing vulnerability. When she talks of her family, the assassinations of her father and husband she becomes passionate. The icy cool slips away. She recovers quickly. An imperfect question or foolish observation from someone near her and she is on them like a terrier, turning their words back in upon them, forcing them on the defensive.

In many ways she reflects the paradoxes in the character of the Sri Lankan. All that gentleness and charm and then, quite suddenly, an explosion. Jehan Perera, educated in both Sri Lanka and at Harvard, is one of the few critical intellectuals able to stand back from and take a cool look at the imperfections of his own land. He thinks, "Sri Lankans are bad at dialogue, at conceptualising and verbalising. Essentially, we find it difficult expressing ourselves. So, often, we brood and then suddenly explode."

When there is one of those explosions it is so often shocking and devastating. In Colombo most people seem curiously unconcerned by the vagaries of war: the battlefield losses, bomb explosions and assassinations as the Tamil Tigers remorselessly pursue their goal of Eelam, which would split their Indian Ocean island in two. There is deep concern for a few days after some particularly dramatic and shocking occurrence.

Perera ruefully observes, "I suppose there has to be an essential weakness in our society when 1000 men can die one day and nothing happens or changes. It is indicative of some terrible failure." Perhaps, on the other hand, it is quite simply the triumph of hope over optimism.

Opposite: **President Kumaratunge at the special Republic Day celebration for HRH The Prince of Wales.**
February 1998.

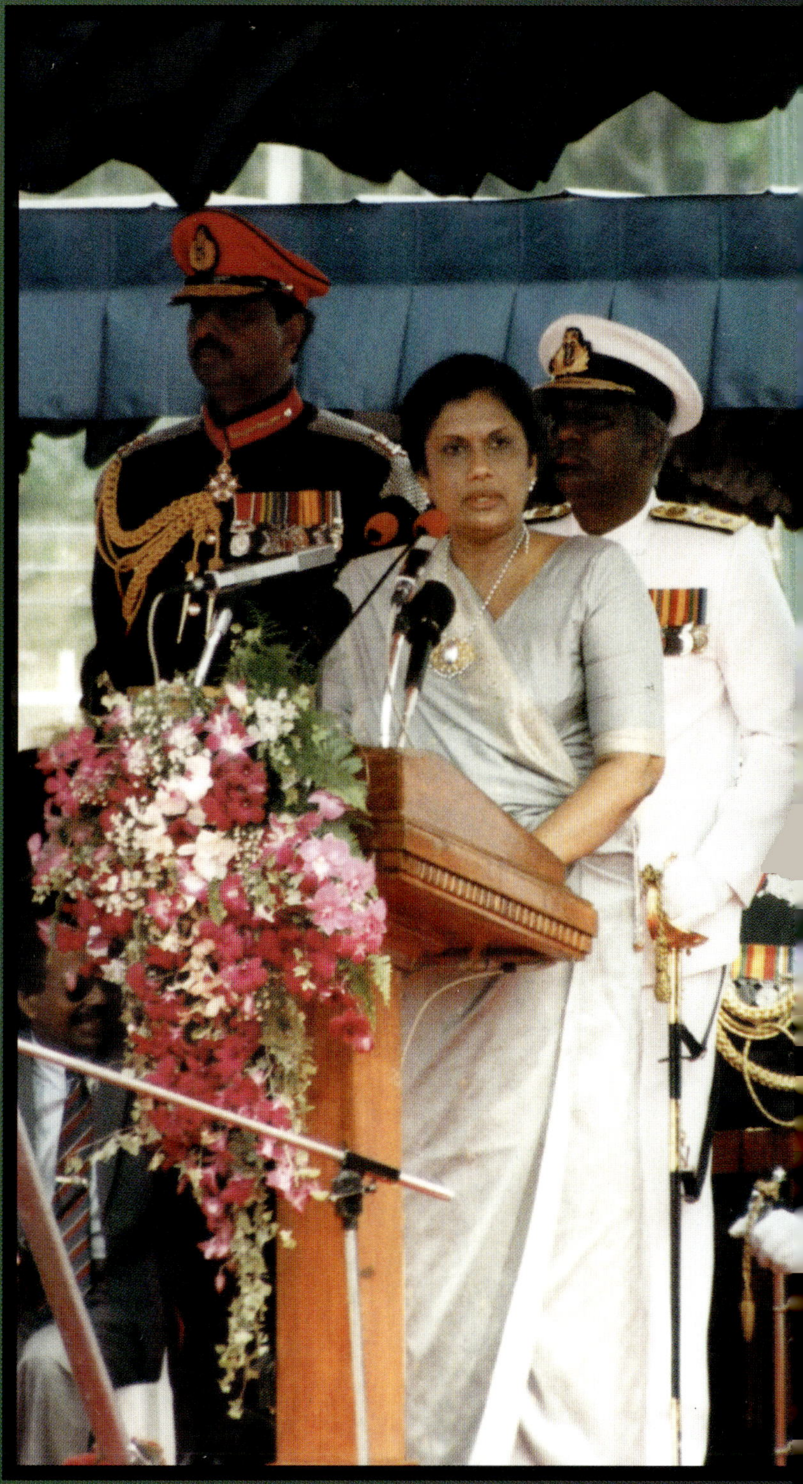

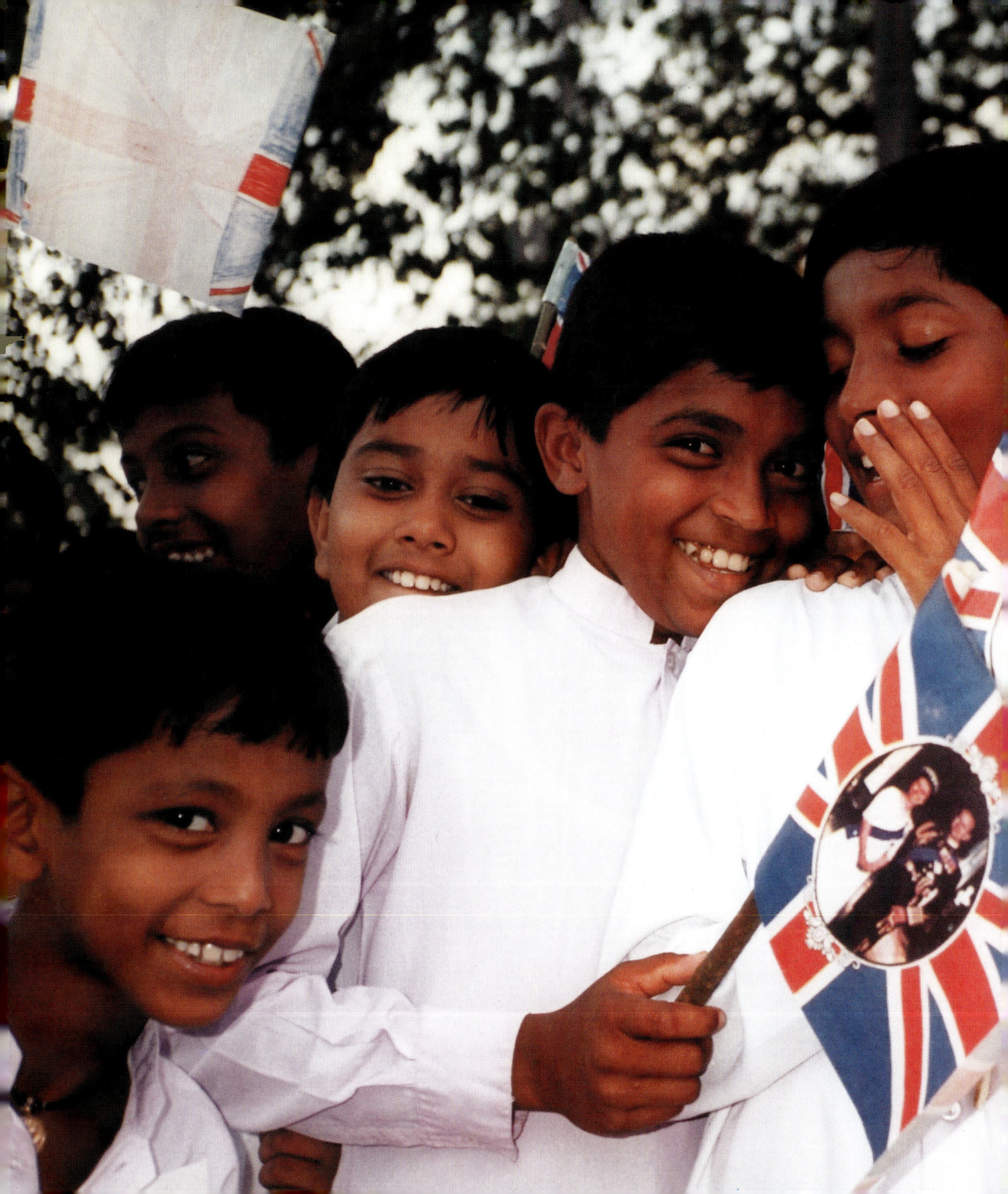

Young fans of the English Royal Family at Kelaniya.

Waiting for the Prince at Kelaniya.

Opposite: The haunted gaze of a young victim of war, Point Pedro Hospital, Jaffna. There were three women in one of the wards: a mother, in her mid-thirties, her 16 year-old daughter and her aunt. The mother was demented. The daughter, poignant beyond belief, bore a perpetually puzzled expression. This was the unmistakable look of a woman who has suffered some terrible, catastrophic wrong. Jaffna, Bosnia, Somalia. The look is the same. The men in uniform came to the door at night. A relatively well to do family, trading in addictive betel leaves, they had gold hidden in the house. On the night of May 19 their house was effectively in No Man's Land between Tigers and army. Their gold was discovered, the women taken outside beaten, raped, genitally mutilated and branded on their foreheads. The LTTE in London announced the women were dead - killed by the army. The army says this disinformation proves the Tigers did this. Army, Tigers or freelances it seemed academic. *June 1996.*

79

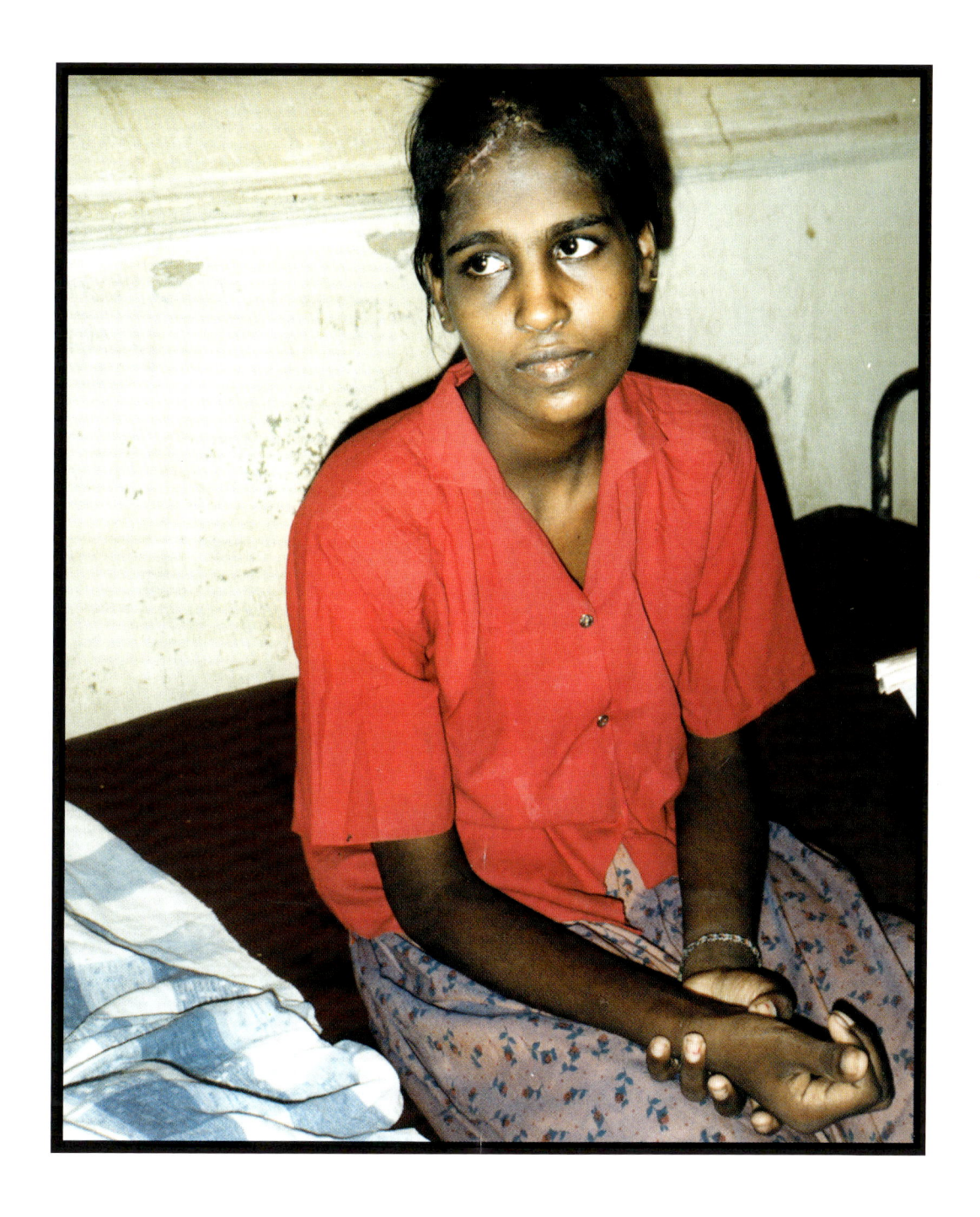

Spot Sergeant Major Kandula at Bandaranaike International Airport, Colombo. He was fed a silver salver of bananas by HRH The Prince of Wales. He is the small Ceylon elephant . . .

Protecting the Prince. An elite commando cradles his Heckler & Koch machine gun.

Election fever in the early evening in Colombo as UNP candidate Maharoof hits the campaign trail. The parliamentary election campaign held in September and October 2000 was bad tempered and frequently bloody. *October 2000.*

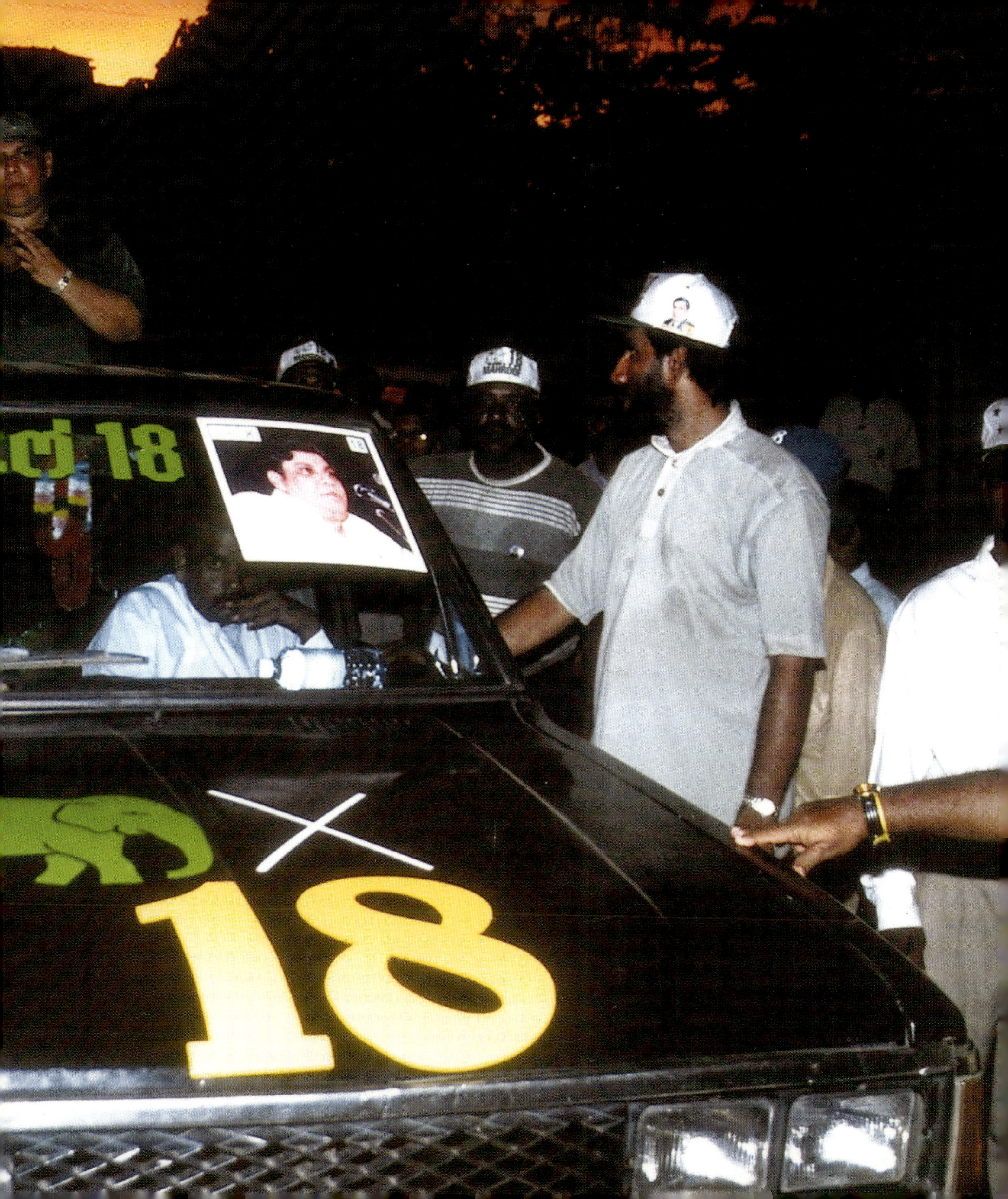
18
18

Riches of the earth. A fruit seller and her son by the roadside near to Kalutara. *February 1997.*

Tough guy. Special Task Force (STF) policeman, Fort, Colombo. *February 1996.*

Stilt fishermen near Ahangama. They perch on the forked branches of trees which have been stuck into the seabed. February 1997.

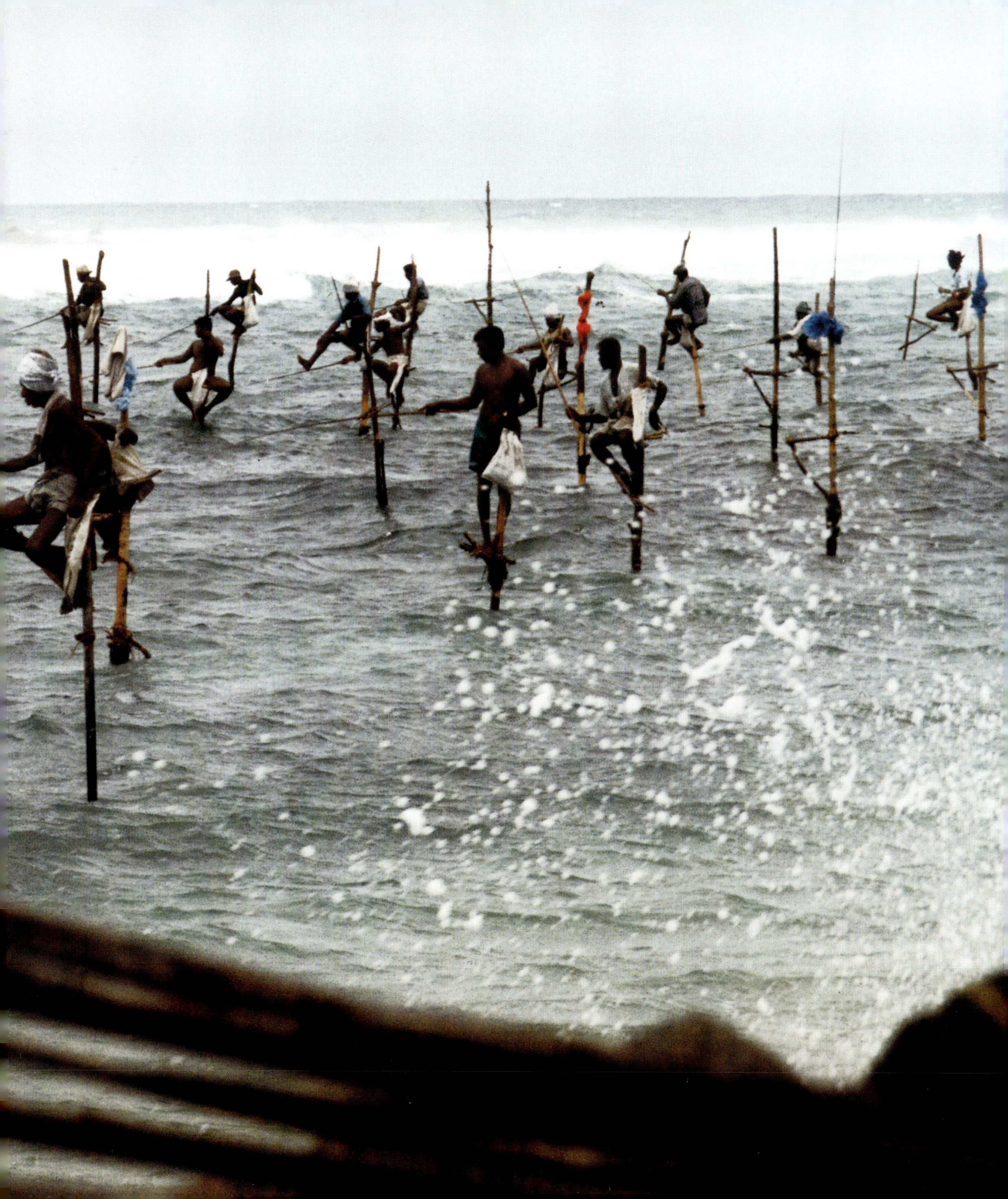

Young boys near Ratnapura.
February 1996.

Opposite: Confidence. SLA soldier Jaffna Town. *October 2000.*

89

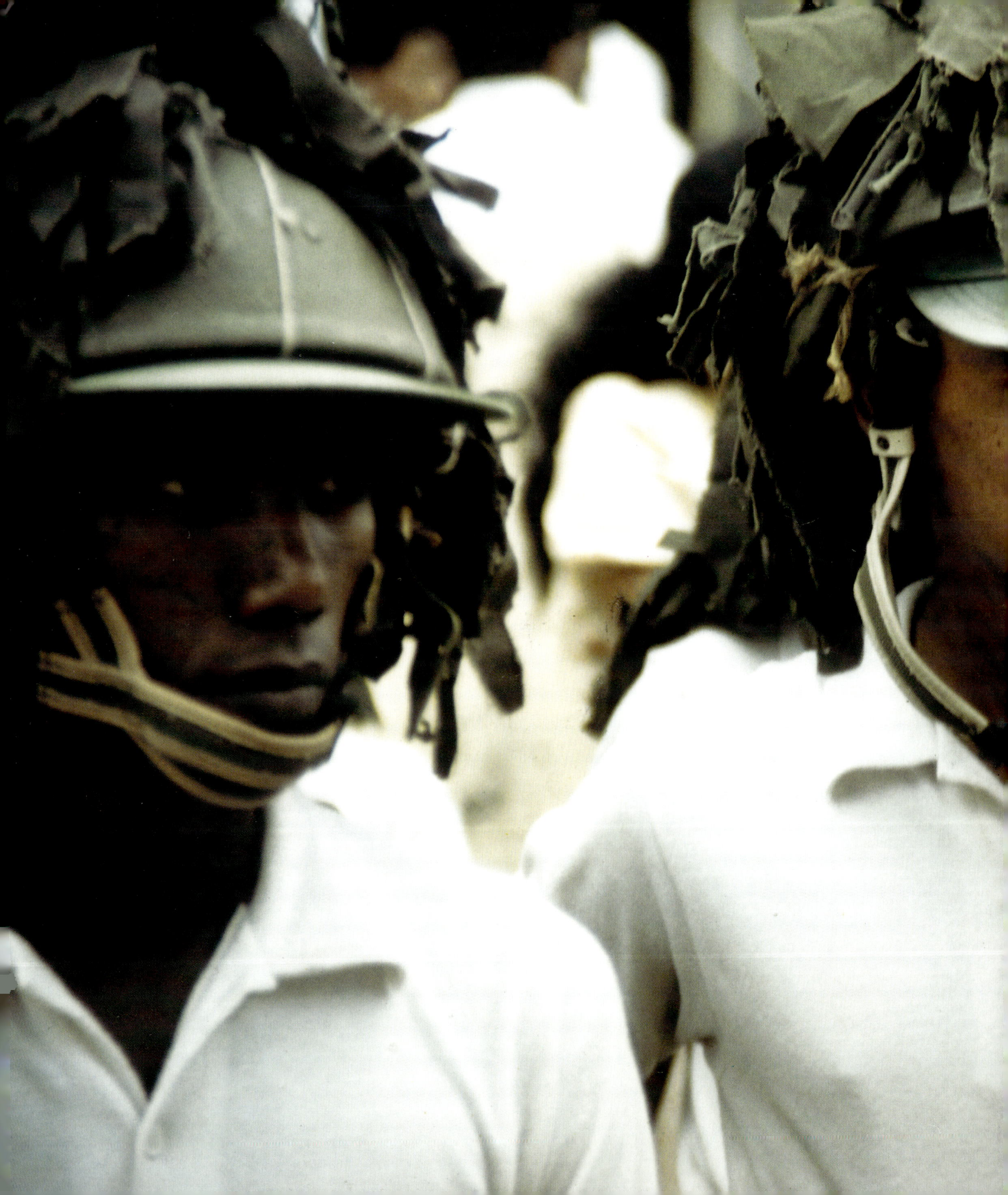

Uncertainty. Young soldier at the scene of the Central Bank blast. *February 1996.*

Picking tea on the Laloocondera Estate in the central highlands. Sri Lanka is the world's biggest exporter of tea. After the coffee blight in the 1840s, Scotsman James Taylor planted the first seedlings for his tea crop in 1847 at Laloocondera and a new industry, now of crucial economic importance to Sri Lanka, was born. *February 1996.*

Opposite: Legal jungle. Signboards of attorneys, Kandy. *March 2001.*

A.B. ALUWIHARE
ATTORNEY-AT-LAW AND
NOTARY PUBLIC
DE SILVA & DE
ATTORNEYS-AT-LAW & NOTA
GAMINI JINASENA
ATTORNEY AT LAW & NOTARY PUBLIC
KINGSLEY FERNANDO
PROCTOR (S.C) & NOTARY PUBLIC
CECIL JAYASINGI
NISHAN DIAS GUNASEKERA
ATTORNEY-AT-LAW & NOTARY PUBLIC
YAMPATHY WICKRAMARATNE
ATTORNEY-AT-LAW
ATTORNEY-AT-LAW & NOTARY
AJITH ROHAN DHARMAPREMA
Attorney-at-Law & N.P.
KITHSIRI SENEVIRATNE
ATTORNEY-AT-LAW-& NOTARY
ERATNE DHARMASE
ATTORNEY-AT-LAW
NDA SENANAYAKE
Attorney-At-Law
PHOTOGRAPHER
SURANGANIE KODITHUWAKKU
ATTORNEY-AT-LAW
& NOTARY PUBLIC

Sixty year-old tusker Raja and his keeper at River Side Elephant Park, Kandy. For many years Raja has been the lead elephant in the annual Kandy Perahera procession. *March 2001.*

Opposite: Public war, private grief. Rally by the Association for the Families of Servicemen Missing in Action outside the City Hall, Colombo. *February 19 1999.*

95

Arthur C Clarke. Prior to the Royal visit to Sri Lanka it was announced that he would receive a knighthood from HRH The Prince of Wales. A journalist for a British tabloid newspaper entered Sri Lanka illegally and concocted a story alleging paedophilia on the part of Clarke, who had lived in Sri Lanka since 1954. Clarke later received his knighthood out of the glare of publicity. *April 1996*

Enduring Images

Mark Twain arrived in Colombo on January 13 1896.

For a few people the lure of the resplendent isle is irresistible. They either become frequent visitors or, indeed, put down roots and stay. Like Arthur C Clarke. He arrived in 1954. Why is he living in Sri Lanka ? "I came here on the way to Australia. Came back. Why did I stay? Thirty-three English winters is the answer, I think. Anyway, where else in the world do people speak English and you are able to support an establishment like this so cheaply?"

Arthur C Clarke - writer, guru, mystic and prophet - doesn't do interviews, he had written to me in Scotland from his home in Sri Lanka. I have the letter to prove it. 'Having done several thousand interviews in all media I'm now completely fed up with talking (even about myself). Everything anyone may need to know will be found in my books . . .'. It was a good evening and goodnight letter.

But there was a ray of hope for the putative interviewer. 'I'm always ready to comment on any major development in my particular areas of interest. Example: an ET landing on the White House lawn, or the first genuine message from space.'

The letter went on to explain that ill health meant that 'I can only manage a 10 hour working day.' Which really doesn't seem so bad for a man then of 77 summers. Pressure is maybe what it's about. 'Even with seven secretaries in three continents, dealing with mail and faxes absorbs so much time that there is very little left for writing . . . Nevertheless if I can conserve my energies, I look forward to greeting 2001.' Well, two weeks and four telephone calls later, I was on Mr Clarke's doorstep in April 1996. I had promised there would be no questions, no interview. I just want to take a photograph. Honest. The photo session was approved. So here I am, sans notebook, Nikon in hand.

The large, modern house in the Sri Lankan capital, Colombo, is in one of the swishest suburbs. Lots of imprtant government chaps live around the corner in a secured zone.

I suppose I am disappointed there are aren't satellite dishes and telescopes sprouting from every orifice but instead here is a spacious, ordered and business-like environment superbly air conditioned. Terrified of being late for the hard won appointment, I'm half an hour early and fully expect to be consigned to some even chillier waiting room.

Instead, I am post haste admitted to the inner sanctum. Arthur C Clarke doesn't look like a living legend. He looks like somebody's suddenly techno-wise grandad seated behind a computer screen. He continues to punch away at the keys and images of the planets flicker on and off.

"With you in a moment. I'm just on Mars." A tiny chihuaha sporting a pink ribbon stirs itself to bark at me. I'm good with dogs so I start to notch up some brownie points. My stock rises even further, I sense, when I present Superman with a copy of one of my own books - "I have a bookcase just for signed copies".

Genial, beaming and welcoming, Arthur C Clarke is just like your favourite grandad and I'm beginning to understand why he doesn't do interviews. It's not just that he's fed up with ill-informed hacks parading the same stupid questions, but you can't get a word in edgeways.

"Mars is the place, you know. That's where it's all going to be happening in the next century. Here on this computer I've got the complete plan for colonisation of the planet." Images shoot up all over the screen. He passes over a copy of his book on Mars, Snows of Olympus. "Do you know Vistapro ? Tremendous computer programme. Done all those pictures, everything on it.

"What I'm really keen on is building an escalator into space. It can de done you know. It would have to be done from the equator so Sri Lanka's the perfect place. There's an ancient rock at a place called Sigyria and that could be used." He hands over a copy of his book *The Fountains of Paradise*, inspired by Sigyria and its stunning 6th century palaces and fortifications.

"Just optioned for a film. We can build it from carbon 60 - you know what that is, of course - now that they've developed a tubular form. You just build it from the equator up to orbit area. Easy really."

You have to remember this is the man who predicted satellites more than half a century ago so I'm not going to attempt to argue about a little matter of an escalator to the stars.

"You know about Operation Insight ?" I don't. "What, you've never heard of it ? The British Government's spending £10 billion on it. Defence Research Establishment you know. Part of the Ministry of Defence. Insight is planning warfare in the 21st century. They were here last week. Now they've sent me this e-mail and I really don't have time to read it. Why don't you read it for me?"

He punches up on the screen a document which is fully 50 pages long. It's the sort of thing that journalists would kill each other, their wives and mistresses to get sight of. Defence tactics in the next century, technophobia, manipulation of the masses. It reads like George Orwell has written it for *The Eagle*. This is Dan Dare dynamite. But I don't have a notebook. Neither can I possibly read or understand this stuff in anything less than 100 hours, ten Clarke working days.

Mr Clarke is off again. "What do you think of this ?" He hands me can the size of your large Baked Bean variety. Written on the side is the legend 'The Great California Earthquake.' Just as soon as it reaches my hand it shakes and vibrates violently. My host collapses in mirth. I've definitely decided he's 77 coming on 7.

"Now you haven't seen my Gold Disc. It's just arrived from Mike Oldfield." A gold disc tumbles from a courier package and is passed across to me. "Please take a picture of me with it. Mike will be so pleased.

"Must confess I've just done an interview. I just couldn't refuse. CNN came here and hooked me up live with Ted Turner by satellite. Wonderful. Now, where were we ? You know, I've got so much in orbit. I can do as much or as little as I want."

Reclining Buddha in the rock temple at Aluvihara.
February 1996.

At the Temple of the Tooth, Kandy as the tooth ceremony begins.
February 1996.

The Mount Lavinia Hotel is one of the great colonial hotels of old Ceylon. Formerly the weekend residence of British Governor Edward Barnes – the present building dates from 1877 – it is said that he was obliged by the British government to sell the magnificent retreat. In London, they failed to appreciate the luxury and expense of this remarkable piece of colonial architecture with its palatial rooms and labyrinthine corridors. Today, it is fully modernised and represents the apogee of luxury. *March 2001*

The Hill Club, Nuwara Elya, looks for all the world like a Home Counties mansion in England with its mock Tudor and stone construction. It was built in 1927 although the Hill Club itself dates from 1876. It still remains as a piece of Olde England in faraway Sri Lanka with its billiard table, library and the mounted heads of wild species which have fallen to the guns of members. Notwithstanding marital hiccups, when I visited in 1996, there was still a picture on the mantelpiece in the withdrawing room of HRH The Prince of Wales with his bride Diana. Certain standards are maintained. A jacket and tie is still required for dinner although you can be provided with the necessary kit from a wardrobe off the butler's pantry. The nights tend to be rather colder in the heights of Nuwara Elya and a club servant will provide you with a hot water bottle when you retire after dinner. Far away Scotland seems rather nearer. It is not just the ambient temperature for there is another sombre reminder. On the wall hangs a reproduction of Sir David Wilkie's *Reading of the Will. February 1996.*

Taprobane Island or, as it is known to the local superstitious stilt fishermen, yakinige dawa, 'The Island of the She-Devil'. The scrub-covered island was bought in the 1930s by the French Count de Mauny who built himself a charming house and created an exotic and beautiful garden.
February 1997.

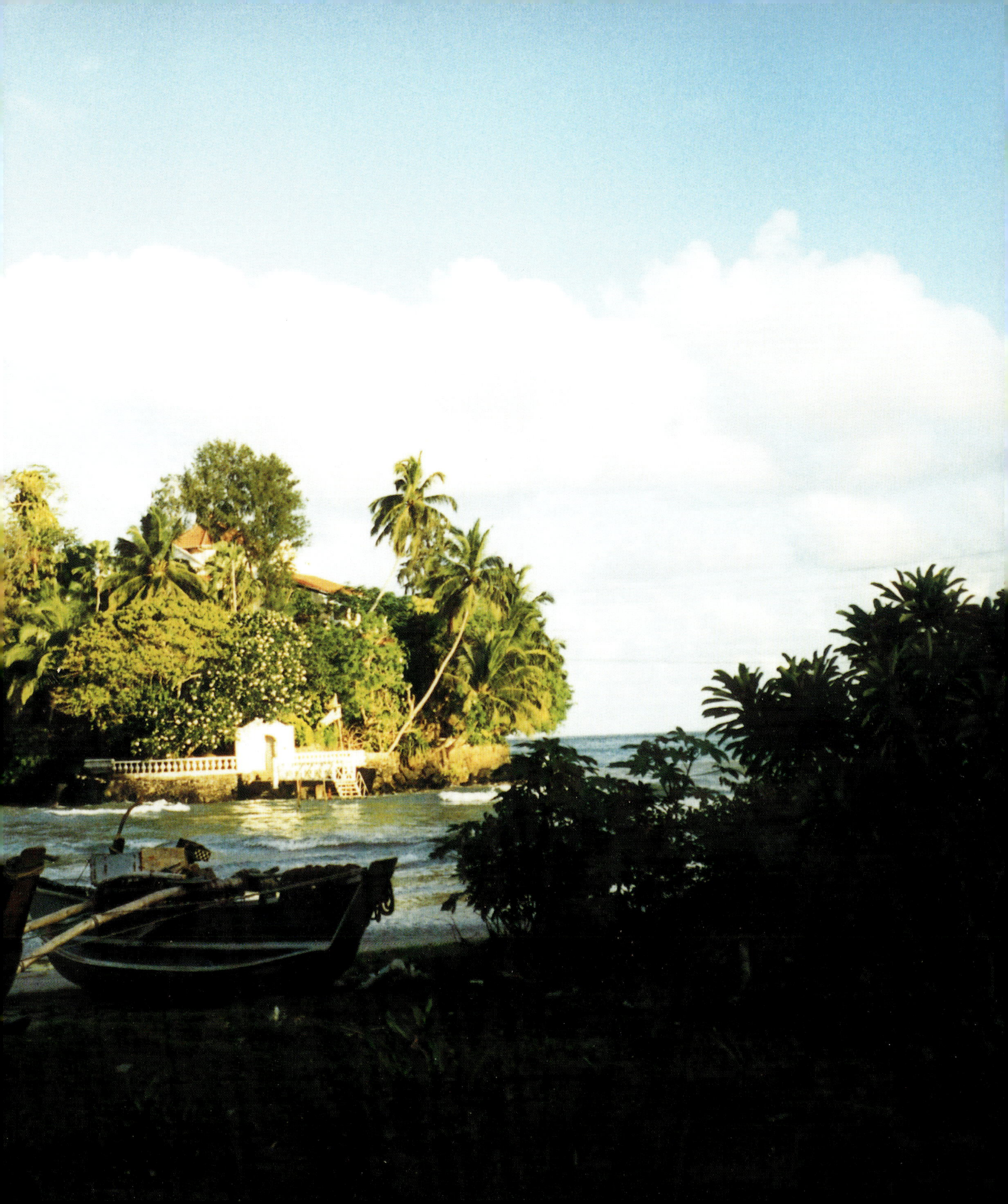

God does not ask for our ability or our inability but our availability. Stone inscription at Adisham House, near Haputale. Now a Benedictine monastery, Adisham was formerly the home of a tea planter from Yorkshire, England. Here he recreated the world of the English country house with a large stone-built residence. *February 1996.*

The temple at Medirigiriya, 39 km. north of Polonnaruwa, is an important 7th century site very much off the tourist track.
February 1999

Schoolboys, Rajgama near Galle. *March 2001*

The sacred Temple of the Tooth, or Dalada Maligawa as it is known, in Kandy was blown up by the Tamil Tigers on January 25 1998, shortly before the official visit of HRH The Prince of Wales. The front of the building was extensively destroyed but, as can be seen from this picture, it has now been expertly and painstakingly restored. *March 2001.*

Stone elephant, Kelaniya.